PROFIT FIRST FOR MICROGYMS

PROFIT FIRST
FOR
MICROGYMS

A SIMPLE SYSTEM
FOR HEALTHY CASHFLOW

BY JOHN BRIGGS

CHERRY CREEK PRESS

Publisher: Cherry Creek Press
Book Design & Typesetting: Chinook Design, Inc.

ISBN (paperback): 978-1-7331790-0-3
ISBN (ebook): 978-1-7331790-1-0

Disclaimer:
The information contained within this book is for informational purposes. It should not be considered legal, financial, or tax advice. You should consult with an attorney or tax professional to determine what may be best for your individual needs.

Incite Tax & Accounting does not make any guarantee or other promise as to any results that may be obtained from using the content within this material. No one should make any financial decisions without first consulting his or her own professional team and conducting his or her own research and due diligence. To the maximum extent permitted by law, Incite Tax & Accounting disclaims any and all liability in the event any information, commentary, analysis, opinions, advice and/or recommendations prove to be inaccurate, incomplete or unreliable, or result in any investment or other losses.

Cherry Creek Press
1618 Cherry Creek Lane
Draper, UT 84020
john@profitfirstformicrogyms.com
801-999-8295

CONTENTS

FOREWORD BY MIKE MICHALOWICZ   VII

CHAPTER 1
YOUR MEMBERS NEED YOU TO BE PROFITABLE   1

CHAPTER 2
THE ULTIMATE ACCOUNTING PARADIGM   17

CHAPTER 3
THE CORE PRINCIPLES OF PROFIT FIRST   35

CHAPTER 4
PRINCIPLE ONE—SMALLER PLATES   45

CHAPTER 5
EAT VEGGIES FIRST   59

CHAPTER 6
REMOVE TEMPTATION   71

CHAPTER 7
EAT SMALLER MEALS MORE FREQUENTLY   81

CHAPTER 8
CASH FLOW ANALYSIS   101

CHAPTER 9
THE LANGUAGE OF BUSINESS   129

CHAPTER 10
GYM TAX STRATEGIES TO INCREASE CASH FLOW   149

CHAPTER 11
TRACKING KEY PREDICTIVE INDICATORS   169

CHAPTER 12
YOUR FIRST YEAR WITH PROFIT FIRST   185

CHAPTER 13
COMMON PITFALLS   195

HEALTH IS PROFIT   207

ACKNOWLEDGMENTS   213

FOREWORD

BY MIKE MICHALOWICZ

IT'S FUNNY IN A NON-FUNNY WAY. I REGULARLY SEE MICROGYM owners put their life and soul into their business, and the business steadily sucks away their life and soul. As I said, funny, in a not-so-funny way.

You run the business, you manage the constant staff turnover, you teach, you serve, you do whatever it takes. And you squeeze all that stuff in, in a mere fourteen-hour workday. Then you repeat it tomorrow. Talk about #Rise&Grind. I think the intention of that hashtag was to get the hard stuff done first. You know, hit the gym first thing. But, for the microgym owner, #Rise&Grind has become a lifestyle. Wake up, grind, grind, and grind some more. Stumble into bed and crawl out tomorrow to repeat.

I suspect you are able to handle hard work. I suspect you can and have risen to the occasion again and again. And ground it out again and again. The problem isn't whether you can work hard (you can and do); it is something different than that. It almost always boils down to financials, or the lack thereof. Most microgym owners that I know suffer from hardships that far outstrip hard work.

Many microgym owners don't take a regular paycheck. At best they have unpredictable pay. And when the business needs the money, the owner is always the first to go without. Profit is non-existent, pay is sporadic, and the financial stress is constant. Can you relate?

And what about your coaches? I can't tell you how many gym owners panic when it comes to paying the coaches. Not paying ourselves, as owners, is painful. But there is nothing worse than not being able to pay the people you rely on most. Does that sound familiar?

The stress goes on and on. No rainy day fund for when the equipment breaks down. No time or funds for the owner to take a real vacation. Not having enough members to support a financially healthy business.

All these financial struggles result in one thing—stress—and lots of it. Extreme work hours of ten, twelve- or fourteen-hour days. A fear of having other people manage the gym, and not being able to afford someone to do that in the first place. The stress is real: You might be unable to sleep or sleep well, feel constant pressure in your chest, have diminishing hope that the business will ever really make it.

But, what if I told you that there is a solution? Not only a solution, but one that is extremely simple and extremely impactful. One that can change it all.

What if I told you that your business already has all the profit it needs? Every financial worry you have is already addressed within your business. And what if I told you it is not about *making* profit, it is about *taking* the profit that is already present in your business?

That is the realization I had for myself in 2008. I had invested in many businesses, including one in the fitness space. My belief was that a good idea backed by extreme relentless effort, brought about financial success. But I was wrong. In 2008 that business and nine others I had started, all collapsed. Business after business failed, even though they were sound ideas, backed by extraordinary effort. The problem was, I didn't understand how money worked. I thought profit and pay and all the money that comes out of the business simply happens on its own. Sell a lot, work a lot, and the money will come. Wrong.

So, in 2008, I created a system for myself. I created a system that allowed me to manage money and make a profit without having to change myself: Profit First. No financial statements. No budgets. No accounting needed. I made a system that allowed me to just be me.

And I think that is the key. It was the key for me and I am convinced it will be a key for you. To have the most success, don't change yourself, change the system around you so that you drive the results you want by continuing to do what you do.

I can't even start to tell you how thrilled I am that you are reading the book that is in your hands now. *Profit First for Microgyms* is the simple system to immediately and permanently make your gym profitable. It is simple, but not necessarily easy. You need to actually do the work. And I can't think of a better person to guide you through this process than John Briggs.

John is not only the leading expert in Profit First for microgyms. John is not only a CPA who understands the tax laws around microgyms. John not only runs his own business, which is financially strong. John is also an extraordinary human being. He is the type of guy who, if you are stuck on a desert island and only could bring one friend, you would pick John. I surely would. John is smart and innovative. John is also caring and understanding. He gets the struggles that you have been through and the future ones you will face and he puts no shame in it. He gets it and will help carry you to financial freedom. Oh, and John owns a CrossFit gym himself. He understands this industry better than anyone I know.

All those past struggles and crazy hours and panics to pay bills are now water under the bridge. We won't waste another second worrying about the past nor beating ourselves up over it. We will focus forward and take profit starting today.

In this book, John has taken the core concepts of Profit First that I created and has tweaked and improved the system specifically for the unique needs of microgyms. He addresses the needs for new equipment, maintenance and repair, paying your coaches, and paying yourself. He shows you how to do all of this, with the side benefit of being a business owner (instead of a business doer). You are about to take home a whole lot more money, and I suspect you'll work less as you do.

As I said, all the profit is already in your business. John is going to show you how to extract it. You couldn't have a better person to help you than John. So, tighten up your (lifting) belt one notch, and let's get to work. John and you are about to make your business permanently profitable.

CHAPTER 1

YOUR MEMBERS NEED YOU TO BE PROFITABLE

WITHIN THE FIRST SIX MONTHS I WAS A PARTNER IN CROSSFIT GSL, it was bleeding cash profusely. Payroll was due. We had to put cash in. Our annual insurance bill arrived. More cash was needed. The CrossFit affiliate fee needed to be paid. Cash. Cash. Cash. I couldn't find a tourniquet fast enough. My business partner and I each put in an additional $12,000 to keep the gym open. This is after I bought in at a value of half of the assets. All that means I didn't buy a business. I hadn't even bought a job. What I had actually bought was debt. Buying half the business gave me the *privilege* of getting to fund half the cash shortfall.

What had I got myself into? This was not the dream I had envisioned.

Over the previous seven years, my firm had consulted, advised, cried with, and celebrated with hundreds of microgym owners on their cash flow. We got their tax burdens down, we helped them identify expenses that weren't productive, we got them implementing the Profit First system. We had proven that we could help gym owners become financially fit. With CrossFit GSL, I saw an opportunity to work in the trenches to see if I could help a failing gym do the same thing we had done for our clients. And, I liked the idea of helping the gym community that I'd been a part of for the last three years by keeping their fitness home available to them.

Boy, I was not expecting the first six months, and how difficult it would be, and how slowly change would happen. Having worked with hundreds of gym owners, I honestly thought it would have been easier to turn a profit in a microgym.

I know my experience isn't completely different from yours and many other boutique and microgym owners. In fact, my experience is probably considered common amongst gym owners. We have a noble dream. We are a group of individuals who have the audacious belief that our services truly change lives. Healthy bodies have a lower risk of diabetes, heart disease, high blood pressure, high cholesterol, and stroke. When our members get more fit and they add more lean body mass while losing fat, we often can confidently say our services are adding time to their existence on Earth. We know that journey is hard, which is why we chose the boutique and microgym model of more individual attention and smaller groups for our members and not the globo-gym model of selling access to equipment for a small monthly rental fee where the quantity of members is the most important part. You'll hear me say this about profit, but it's the same truth for health. A healthy business is a profitable business and that business can have a million dreams. A business with zero profit can only have one dream. Our noble dream is connected to helping others have endless possibilities for their own dreams.

That is what inspired us to risk gym ownership. But, frustratingly, we ended up buying ourselves a job (or worse, debt) instead of a business. And for the time we put in, it was a really low-paying, hourly rate job.

Did you open your gym to become an entrepreneur? And, given your love for fitness, it made sense that you would try your hand at being a gym owner. Did you think it would be so cool to just work out all day? So gym ownership seemed like the best option for that. Did you feel a call to gym ownership, a greater force inspiring you to move forward? Were you looking to help people not feel alone? You wanted to build a supportive community, one that would inspire them to a healthier, happier life. As Michael Gerber calls it in his classic business book, *E-Myth*, did you have an entrepreneurial seizure? As an excellent coach, did you know you could run a business better than the gym where you were working? Did you simply just want to be able to coach forever? And by being a gym owner, you took control over the ability to do that. Was your only goal to help people live longer?

Our noble purpose spurs us into action. When things don't play out the way they did in our minds, our motivations can carry us through the tough times. However, this "purity of purpose" can also lead us to believe that we don't deserve to be profitable. We tell ourselves, "I'm not in it for the money."

If it so happens that we end up having profit (by accident) and are able to upgrade our lifestyle a little bit, it's just a happy consequence of owing the gym. It's acceptable. However, if we ever consciously focused on turning a profit, now we have corrupted our purpose. It's as if to say we become tarnished individuals and are now on a slippery slope of becoming a corrupt business owner, the type you hear about in the news that take advantage of workers and prey on the weak. This cannot be further from the truth.

You deserve to be profitable and when you follow the action steps in this book, that's exactly what you will experience.

REWRITING STORIES

On one family vacation we took our four kids to Disneyland. On this trip I thought a lot about the history of Disneyland. Many argue that the popularity of Disneyland is due to Disney's movies. With a good movie, Disney makes a lot of money.

But a good movie does much more than just make money for Disney. It also generates interest for people to meet their new favorite characters and buy toys or trinkets of those favorite characters. That got me thinking about the stories of some of Disney's older fairy tales. Most of Disney's stories are rooted in older versions that are often dark and gruesome.

The original story of *Sleeping Beauty* is from 1634 and was titled *Sun, Moon, and Talia* by Giambattista Basile. Yes, the princess pricked her finger on a splinter of poisonous flax. But then the original story took a much different turn than the Disney version.

A king wanders across the princess's sleeping body and... well... the princess, while still asleep, gives birth to twins. Feel free to fill in the part I left out. As I said, dark and gruesome.

3

Later, one of the twins sucks the splinter from the princess's finger and wakes her up. The princess ends up marrying the king, who happened to burn his first wife alive so that he could be with the princess.

But wait there's more! Before the king burned his wife, the queen tried to kill the twins and serve them to the king to eat. Good grief! Very different from the Disney version. (I like the Disney version better).

With many of its movies, Disney spun the story differently from the originals, and the Disney version often leaves us feeling happy.

Both the dark and gruesome original story and Disney's version of *Sleeping Beauty* are just stories. It's like when you are telling a story, and your spouse jumps in and says, "that's not how I remember it." You each have different versions. So it is with many stories. Each has many versions. What version of our story are we telling ourselves? The stories we tell ourselves are often more powerful than we imagine.

For example, have you ever found yourself saying things such as:

- I'm ok that there is no money in this business because I'm serving a greater purpose.
- People are cheap and they won't pay my rates.
- It's really just a hobby I'm passionate about. I don't even want to be paid.
- I just need ten more members.
- Numbers just aren't my thing. I'm not an accountant and I'll never understand this stuff.
- My members will think I'm greedy if they find out the gym is a very profitable business.
- There's no money in this business anyway.
- I'm just here to help people.

These are all just stories and they can be changed, thank goodness, because those are real turds of stories. This book will help you change the story. Here are some ways to rewrite the turd stories into better stories.

- When I make money, I can serve more people.
- I value what I do, and so do my members. They will pay our rates.
- I'm so grateful that I get paid good money to do something I'm so passionate about.
- I control my cash flow and will figure out how to be profitable with my current number of members.
- I may not understand accounting stuff yet. But I'm ready to learn what I need to because I'm more than capable of getting this.
- I deserve to be profitable because profit will allow me to serve my purpose.
- My members deserve that I be profitable because then I can enhance their experience.

Those are better stories. The rewritten statements make you feel better. You wouldn't say to a member as a form of encouragement, "You'd probably be able to lift more if your form didn't suck," because you know that negative approach won't work. Don't use a negative approach with your stories either. Rewrite them. Be positive. Know that you deserve to be profitable. When you change the story about your business and your gym's profitability, you actually make it possible to continue to do your noble work.

THE HALF OF GYMS FAIL STORY

Have you heard this story before? Fifty percent of new gyms fail within the first three years. That goes to 80 percent in the first five years. These claims are supposedly based on many much data—From the Statistic Brain Research Institute in 2017, for example and from IHRSA (International Health, Racquet & Sportsclub Association)[1] to

---

[1] Statistic Brain, "Startup Business Failure Rate By Industry," May 5, 2017, https://www.statisticbrain.com, accessed November 24, 2019

Jim Schmaltz, "Why Most Startup Fitness Studios Fail," Aug 27, 2018, https://ihrsa.org, accessed November 24, 2019

name just two. Those numbers very possibly can be true. I have no reason to believe otherwise. And I say, who cares?

I'm not saying that in the naïve way thinking that bad things can't happen to me. Or that I'm so much smarter than everyone else, and clearly those failed gyms were owned by people not as smart as me. There is no doubt that I'm a friggin' idiot. (As I write this, my wife is nodding in firm agreement.) I also know that bad things can happen to me. The reason I don't care about the fail rate of gyms is because it isn't going to change how I behave. I'm sure you've heard a similar statistic before, but you still opened your gym. So it didn't frighten you. You heard this story and went forward anyway. I have found gym owners to be more fearless than any other group of entrepreneurs.

The fail rate of gyms is a story. One based on data, sure. But it's still a story. Wouldn't it benefit me more to believe my story is one of accomplishment? And I'm not talking about *The Secret* type of approach, where if I just believe my gym will be successful, it will automatically happen. I'm talking about a way in which the belief of success shapes my decisions and focus. A profitable gym that you and your members deserve is your new story.

HARD WORK IS HIDING THE PROBLEM

Profit is the only way to secure your efforts in pursuing your purpose. What *is* profit? Profit is what is left over after you receive cash for the services you offer and then send out cash for your expenses. Without cash left over, without profit, you will work hard, really hard. That happens to be the easiest and most common way for someone to cover up the fact their business is unhealthy.

Take our client, Kat, for instance. For years she told herself, "Just ten more members." She told herself that at fifty members. Then at sixty members. Then at eighty members. Even at one hundred members. Each time, she said, "Just ten more members." Her microgym was no more profitable at one hundred members than it was at fifty members. But how much more work was she doing? Fifty more members meant more classes that needed to be coached. Because she didn't have the cash flow to hire any new coaches, she took on those classes herself. Her workday expanded to include more hours. Twice as many members meant double the customer service time commitment. Also, while it doesn't show up immediately, she accelerated the wear and tear on her equipment that she now has to replace sooner even though, for some reason, with twice as many members, there isn't any more cash available to do that. But dammit if she didn't work her tail off the best way she knew how! And she was able to keep her gym open for years before finding Profit First.

If the momentum of an unhealthy business doesn't change, eventually bills will come due, coaches will stop working because they aren't getting paid, quality of life deteriorates into survival mode, houses get foreclosed, landlords or banks change the locks on the gym doors. Hard work can slow down this reality, but never prevent it or magically make it disappear. Combining hard work and profit on the other hand, now we are getting somewhere.

Without profit, our hard work blends our days together into a jumbled memory where serving our purpose isn't a possibility because we are only capable of focusing on survival. If we just hold on a little longer, if we work a little harder, stay up a little later, something great is going to happen to us.

We have to rewrite that story. I'm not going to be trite and say, "Work smarter, not harder." You are working really hard and you are going to need to continue to work hard to turn the ship around. And (not but), you can take action doing all this book will ask of you and you *will* find profitability. The story should be: Work hard *and* work smart with a proven cash flow system.

To clarify, "making a profit" is a different concept than "getting paid."

What do I mean?

You work in your gym; maybe you do the marketing campaigns, maybe you are coaching some or all the classes, maybe you clean the gym, or maybe you manage the inventory you are trying to resell. Those are tasks that you could pay someone else to do.

So because you are doing them, you should at least pay yourself what you would have paid someone else to do the same task. That is getting paid for working in your business.

That is not the same thing as making a profit. Making a profit is what you get because you are the gym owner. Making a profit is your return on investment for being the one taking the risk of owning the business. If you do not make a profit, that means your business is not retaining any cash from its sales. It means your gym's sustainability could be one of those 50 percent of failed businesses. If your gym is not profitable, you will not be able to serve your "why" for very long. That *is* the tragedy of any failed business.

YOUR PURPOSE NEEDS TO BE PROFIT

You set out on your journey believing you were going to be successful. That you would accomplish your noble purpose, the reason you got into business. I know this because no one ever said, "I'm going to open a gym so that I can waste years of my life, losing money I don't have, to be farther from any semblance of freedom than when I started." Instead you had a purpose: to provide a community of support for others, to help others be healthier and happier through fitness, to coach in your style without someone telling you how to do things, and the list of noble motivations can go on and on. There are countless other purposes one may have when opening a gym.

Understanding your purpose in doing anything is a critical factor in whether you will find success or not. With the popularity of Simon Sinek's book *Start With Why*, I believe this idea of finding purpose and finding your "why" has become super cliché.

Everybody thinks they are an expert in it. Well, they aren't. I'm certainly not. However, I do know that when I understand the reason why I'm doing something, I've given myself a better chance of success. So what is your reason for being a gym owner?

You have your very unique, only true for you, sole purpose, your true "why" in being a microgym owner. The noble motivation that you experience is likely different from mine, which is totally fine. Keep yours. I'll keep mine. Use yours. I'll use mine.

You can pursue your noble purpose and at the same time pursue being profitable. Being a microgym owner is not about *either* being lucrative and making money *or* changing lives and people. It is about both. You deserve to fulfill your purpose and, at the same time, you deserve to be rewarded with a profit.

In fact, from a rubber hitting the road standpoint, you have to have the purpose of making a profit. I repeat, one purpose of business has to be to make a profit. There is no other way to accomplish our noble pursuits without it. Focusing on profit will *not* take anything away from your special "why."

THE PUMPKIN PLAN PLUS PROFIT FIRST

My "why" for gym ownership developed like an eighteen-wheeler. It started slow, but now that it's up to speed, it's going to be hard to stop this semitruck.

My CrossFit "why" started in 2011, when I was introduced to the founder of the 321go Project, Clay Weldon. 321go was offering a mentoring program which, at the time, was headed by Chris Cooper. After I proved my worth as a tax genius, 321go Project asked if I would be willing to give a financial education session to their mentoring clients. My approach to bringing on new clients for the accounting firm is to educate the crap out of them. It's the "be so good they can't ignore you" approach, and we made it obvious that we know what we are talking about and we can save them a lot of money in tax savings. This approach often led to the person hiring us. 321go wanted to get me in front of a gym owner willing to spend at least thirty minutes on financial education? Sign me up.

I came up with a thirty-minute financial personal training session and 70 percent of those gym owners hired our firm to provide tax or accounting services. That was my exposure to microgyms for the next couple of years.

During this time, I read *The Pumpkin Plan* by Mike Michalowicz. In that book, he provides action steps and resources to help any business owner identify profitable and enjoyable clients they want to work with. It just so happens that pumpkin farmers who grow ginormous pumpkins provide a great metaphor and framework for that. Doing his exercises made me realize that my microgym owner clients were some of my favorite clients. They were respectful. They understood the value we were providing them and they actually listened to our advice. I wanted more of them. If I could duplicate them I would.

So we started focusing our marketing efforts on getting in front of microgym owners. Up to this point, I only knew the business side of it. What gym owners actually did inside the gym was still not clear. My impression was that it was a training regimen to create more Chuck Norris's. For the people who say, "You want me to do an air squat? You mean push the earth down with my legs." The type that can finish a twenty-minute AMRAP in five minutes. Is that a tractor you just threw over your head?

The first workout I witnessed was at a gathering of CrossFit affiliates in Park City, Utah. I felt as if I was in a car accident. I was present the whole time but unsure of what I was witnessing. When asked about it later, my only response was, "Well there was a big, loud sound. My body was contorted; I'm pretty sure I heard something snap and tear. And when I came to, I was lying sprawled out on the ground." I didn't even do the workout. I just watched. Still, it was enough for me to realize that if I'm going to help microgym owners, I needed to try out the product.

I immediately hated it and loved it at the same time. I loved that I could just show up and they would tell me what to do. I didn't have to make any decisions. One of the first benefits I noticed was the sense of confidence it gave me throughout the day. In every workout I was asked to push myself. The mental strength that comes from pushing myself daily stays with me through the parts of my day when I need to work on my business. No one is going to make the tough decisions for me.

So I continued working on my fitness and studying the business of gym ownership. I also continued to improve my accounting firm, which is how I found *Profit First* also by Mike Michalowicz. The time put into learning helped me see signs that the gym where I was a member might not be profitable. A not-profitable gym is on borrowed time. I got involved because I liked the people I worked out with. I had established a fitness routine that worked for me and I didn't want to try to figure out something new and I also wanted the challenge of seeing whether Profit First would help this gym become profitable and sustainable.

I put my money where my mouth is and bought half of the business. I want the community to continue so it can support those who need that in their life. I want the coaches to have a place to help people become healthier and happier. I want to prove that Profit First can work in my gym, because then it will surely work in all gyms.

IS THERE A *MOST* IMPORTANT THING FOR YOUR BUSINESS?

Why you get up in the morning; how you do things at your gym; how you mentor your coaches and other team members; and when, where, and how you expand your empire are all secondary to your finances. None of these things will mean as much, or in some cases even be possible, if you don't have a healthy cash flow and a good accounting system.

There are a craptastic amount of opinions about what is the most important thing in business:

- You're only as strong as the team surrounding you.
- Your culture is the only thing that matters.
- You can't succeed without excellent relationships.
- You need a strong mission and vision if you want to be successful.
- Put people first.
- It's sales.
- No, it's marketing.
- No, it's leadership.

The real answer is profitability. If you are profitable, you can do whatever you want. If you aren't profitable, the only thing that matters is getting to profitability.

What does profitability mean? Profitability is just a term. It's a concept. Profitability doesn't mean uber rich. It could, but it doesn't have to. Profitability just means that, after cash comes into the gym by selling services and products and the gym pays for all its expenses (which includes paying you market rate when you work in the gym), there is money left over that isn't spoken for.

If that ends up being one dollar, it's still profitable. In the early months of owning CrossFit GSL, we worked hard to just get to at least one dollar of profitability. But one dollar of profitability wasn't our end goal. It was just the goal at the time. Growing the business so that it provided a return on our time and investment was the goal. Hitting that goal means we created value and a great experience for our members so that value could be returned to us in the form of compensation.

PROFIT FIRST UNCOVERS YOUR ISSUES

Working the Profit First system helps you uncover the issues that are holding the gym back from profitability or from more profitability. Sometimes it's hard to know how big the problem is just by making a blanket statement that there is not enough profit in the business.

A few months after officially being a microgym owner, during my normal morning workout, I noticed a small wet spot about six inches in diameter on the floor.

"We need to tell the landlord about this." The roof is his responsibility in our lease agreement. Well, we didn't do that fast enough.

Two weeks later, we had a freak downpour, the kind of downpour that soaks through clothes then through skin then through bones in about three seconds. The rain only lasted about thirty minutes. But thirty minutes was enough time. Water leaked from the roof with the kind of pressure and volume you get when you turn on a fire hydrant.

It would seem the small wet spot from two weeks earlier was trying to communicate to me that a much bigger problem existed. When the flood actually came, the bigger problem revealed itself, and it was too late to fix it. Now we were playing reactively to the problem instead of being proactive.

A lack of profit in a business is like a small wet spot. It is trying to communicate to us that bigger problems exist. Don't ignore it as we did our wet spot. This book is going to help you identify the bigger problems behind the small financial wet spots.

Étienne Booth owns the microgym Engrenage in Canada. Early on, he knew that he didn't want to end up a slave to the gym, but he still felt as though he needed to "eat last" because it would be selfish to pay himself and to say, "this is mine."

"I felt a mix of being lost and being selfish," he told me. "I didn't know how to transform myself so the gym could be what it needed to be for my members, the coaches, and myself."

The challenge didn't end with just his own mindset. The others who had a voice in the gym resisted strongly when he began implementing Profit First. But wait, there's more! His accountant pushed back because, "profit is always going to be what's left over; you can't change that."

Sorry Mr. Typical Accountant, but you *can* change that. It is in your control, and Étienne took that control and pushed through the resistance. Profit First gave him freedom from becoming a slave to his gym.

"Profit First taught me how to say 'no' by prioritizing the right things instead of trying to please everyone," he said.

You know what happens when members or coaches suggest you bring in new equipment or start a new program or add a new bathroom or... The list never ends, and it's really easy for others to spend your money. By letting the Profit First system work, Étienne was able to determine when he should say no.

In the first four quarters running Profit First, he started with taking 3 percent of his income for profit and each quarter increased it so that by the fourth quarter he was setting aside 15 percent of his revenue for profit. He also had enough to pay back the remaining amount on the $40,000 business loan he took out to start his gym. Profit First has become a self-improving method for him. If his profit increases, then he's improving. If revenue increases, then he's improving.

"The greatest impact that Profit First has had for me is to break the belief that profit is simply what is left after expenses. So, instead of having the mindset that I need to reinvest to make the gym big in order to generate profit, the system switched my mentality and allowed me to grasp the concept that, in order to better my business, profit needs to happen right now."

PROFITABILITY REQUIRES WORK AND YOU CONTROL IT

One thing I love about our human existence is that we are in control. I have no one else to blame for my failures or my successes but myself. So sincerely… thank you for taking control and making the time to not only read this book, but also implement the Profit First system. I know that when you apply what you learn from this book, your gym will be transformed and more importantly, your life will as well.

What I'm going to teach you is going to be simple. It can be easy to discount ideas when they seem simple. Simple isn't the same as easy. Following through seems to be the hard part. The story you control is that follow through doesn't have to be hard. Profit First works. I've been using it in my business since 2015, and my bank account balances are up, my take-home pay is healthy, and I don't stress out about paying bills or payroll anymore.

Mike Michalowicz has a saying that I've repeated so many times, I didn't realize I got it from him: Cash flow is the life blood of your business. I'll say this a lot in this book, and eventually, you'll start saying it all the time too. It doesn't matter if you have the best coaches, the cleanest gym, the best onboarding systems, and the best members. If your business has no cash, it will not survive. Create value, and cash comes in. But it isn't enough. You need boundaries around your cash as it comes into your business. This entire book will help you protect that cash flow.

Taking control over protecting your cash flow is something that is most definitely in your power. When you do that, your noble motivation will take its place in the world and come to fruition. Without cash, your gym will die. If you want to be able to help others with their fitness goals; if you want to own a business and not a job; if you want freedom to work only when you want to; if you want to build a culture for your gym members; if you want to provide a great life for your coaches and members, then offer the right selection of services for your members, charge the right amount for those services, have fewer expenses than what you bring in, and enjoy a healthy cash flow. Having that will allow you to serve the people you set out to help *and* you will be profitable. That's a good story to have.

FINANCIAL WORKOUT

It's time to get honest with the stories you are telling yourself. If you aren't one hundred percent convinced that you can pursue your noble motivation *and* be profitable (yes, both of them at the same time), take the time to rewrite that story. In fact, email me why you deserve to be profitable and what motivates you. Send your email to john@ProfitFirstForMicrogyms.com and put in the subject line "I deserve to be profitable." I want to hear from you! This simple exercise may help you uncover mental blocks you didn't know you had.

This book provides you with a lot of resources which you can find at www.ProfitFirstForMicrogyms.com/tools. While seeing the list of tools may make more sense after I introduce them throughout the book, you may be so excited to get started that you want to check them out right now. So go for it!

CHAPTER 2

THE ULTIMATE ACCOUNTING PARADIGM

I N 1876, THE SCORING SYSTEM FOR FOOTBALL WAS CREATED AT the Massasoit Convention. In that first scoring system, a successful field goal try was rewarded with five points, while touchdowns and the conversions were each worth four points. Fast forward to 2019; now a successful field goal is only three points with a touchdown earning six points and a conversion is only worth one.

Why the change? Kicking a successful field goal was thought to be very difficult back in 1883. Well, it turns out kicking a field goal is much easier than scoring a touchdown. I'm also willing to bet the people back in 1883 never imagined anyone being able to kick field goals fifty yards or longer.

Before the world became electronic, it was a paper world. My mom always likes to tell me the story of "back in the day" when she worked at Smith and Barney's. She would have gigantic spreadsheets made of graph paper taped together in order to track the sales of the various locations within the company. In retail stores, they didn't get an electronic receipt of the transaction happening or the customer paying. Instead a customer would use actual cash to pay for an item. A simple sale of something that cost five dollars would require the customer to give a five-dollar bill to the store clerk, and then they would walk out with the item.

Maybe that store clerk would or would not record the sales info into the cash register. If the store clerk did punch the info into the cash register to record the sale, the cash register would make a cha-ching sound. On the other hand, if the store clerk pocketed the five dollars, then there would be no record of the sale, and it was very difficult for the store owner to know that five dollars had been stolen.

So store owners changed the price. Instead of five dollars, it was now $4.99. Now the store clerk *had* to punch the information into the cash register so that a penny could be returned to the customer. The sale was now recorded, the cash register cha-chinged, the owner in the back room could hear a sale was made, and the chance of that money getting stolen was greatly reduced.

There is no need for that type of pricing today when money can be transferred electronically. Yet, you still see prices ending in anything but zero. Those who have studied pricing methodologies cannot explain why, they just know the evidence supports that this pricing model leads to more sales.

But the two reasons are very different. One was for anti-theft, and the other is for customer manipulation.

Why the history lesson on field goal scoring and 99 cent pricing?

Both are paradigms, and paradigms have a massive effect on our behaviors.

Bob Proctor (he is the Law of Attraction teacher popularized by the movie *The Secret*) provides the best definition I've found for paradigms. "A paradigm is a collection of beliefs held by a group of people. It's not just one belief held by one person. These beliefs are shared, passed on and believed by generations." In other words, paradigms are stories we collectively choose to believe in.

Religious beliefs, your favorite political party, racism, how much money you should make, if you think CrossFit is the best idea ever or the worst idea ever, how many points should a field goal be worth, and why to set prices ending in 99 cents are all examples of paradigms.

In Chapter 1, I emphasized that we have the power to rewrite any of our own stories. In this chapter, I want to share some of the money paradigms (stories) you may or may not have that also deserve a rewrite. The way we view, think about, and use money shows up in every aspect of our gyms. We need to make sure that we are not telling ourselves the story that our noble purpose in opening a gym would be tainted if we make too much money.

WHAT YOU'VE HEARD ABOUT MONEY GROWING ON TREES IS WRONG

Have you ever been told that money doesn't grow on trees? This was a common response I got growing up when I would ask for something from my parents or when a new sports season would start, and I needed to get new shoes and equipment. My mom or dad (they were united on this point) would say "Money doesn't grow on trees," either as a *no* response or as a way to tell me they would purchase the crap I wanted but they weren't happy about having to spend their money.

My parents were teaching me a paradigm that had been passed down to them. I know their intention was to teach me that money is earned from hard work. But the unintended message of "money doesn't grow on trees" is that money is a scarce resource. It is limited and if one person has money, then there is less money for you and also that it's hard to get more money. If it grew on trees it would be easier to get it.

I, of course, *mistakenly* believed them. I know that makes me sound crazy. But I don't believe it anymore. Now, do I think that actual, literal dollar bills grow on trees? No.

What does grow on trees? Not the physical, literal, dollar bill. But don't apples grow on trees? Don't lemons grow on trees? And can't I sell apples and lemons for money? So wouldn't that mean that money grows on trees?

You could use the tree itself to make wood, or paper. Bamboo trees have been used to make bedsheets and blankets. Trees can also be used to make furniture, or decorations, or canoes or boats. Melaleuca trees produce oil. Heck, even the first two people, Adam and Eve, used tree leaves to cover their nakedness as Eve sported humankind's first-ever miniskirt. Aren't wood and paper sold for money? We buy furniture, decorations, bedsheets and blankets, clothing, and oil, right?

Money *does* grow on trees.

The belief that money doesn't grow on trees is a blueprint my parents taught me. I'd say, "Dad, can I get a new pair of shoes? This giant hole in the heel is making my foot bleed." My parents would respond with: "You think money grows on trees?" I learned that I shouldn't ask to improve things that are old and worn down.

So, when that rower or bike needs replacing, am I going to tell my members that their experience doesn't matter because money doesn't grow on trees? Or that equipment won't be replaced just because it's old and worn down? Because I believe that money doesn't grow on trees, will I stay with status quo? Will I tell myself that I should be happy working fifteen-hour days and sleeping on the couch at the gym, because I can't afford to even rent a one room apartment? After all, I was taught making money has to be hard. Will I convince myself that I shouldn't expect to be profitable? Do you see how this paradigm is holding back many from realizing they deserve to be profitable? (Maybe even you.)

"Money doesn't grow on trees" is just one example of an incorrect paradigm. All of us are exposed to countless opinions from mentors, coaches, the media, the government, well-intentioned parents, people who work so hard at appearing successful, and the advertising industry that has spent billions on studying our psychology; the list goes on and on.

Not everything we hear is true. Shocker, I know. But man, once we accept an opinion as truth, our brains are very stubborn. Have you ever heard of "Confirmation Bias"? It's our tendency to cling to information that supports our belief and reject anything that doesn't. In the late 70s, a pair of Standard studies uncovered this issue. This finding has been confirmed by thousands of other researchers.[1] Not

---

[1] Thomas Shultz, Jacques Katz, Mark Lepper; "Clinging to Beliefs: A Constraint-satisfaction Model," http://www.psych.mcgill.ca, accessed November 24, 2019

Kitty Xu, Brian Anderson, Erik Emeric, Veit Stuphorn, Steven Yantis, Susan Courtney; "Neural Basis of Cognitive Control over Movement Inhibition: Human fMRI and Primate Electrophysiology Evidence," https://www.cell.com, Dec 7, 2017, accessed November 24, 2019

Bret Stetka, "The Neuroscience of Changing Your Mind," *Scientific American,* December 7, 2017

Elizabeth Kolbert, "Why Facts Don't Change Our Minds," *The New Yorker,* February 19, 2017

all hope is lost though. We have the ability to change our beliefs, our habits, our stories.[2]

If we are presented evidence that one of our belief's is wrong, we can totally change our mind. None of us are perfect. I, for sure, am not. I know this because my wife tells me all the time: "Hey, you aren't perfect." We all have beliefs that could be holding us back, and these limiting beliefs can often negatively affect our business decisions. Your gym can never grow past your beliefs, so we need to re-write any financial paradigms or stories that are holding back the legacy you can leave to the world.

RE-WRITING MONEY-RELATED PARADIGMS

We don't know what we don't know. So let's go over these paradigms that are related to accounting, how much money we need, and profit. We'll start with accounting paradigms:

"Accounting is a necessary evil." Geez! That sounds like a prison sentence; you are stuck having to do something even though you hate it. We can never get excited about something if we think it's evil. Accounting is necessary. When approached properly, your accounting efforts will produce financial statements that give you insights into your cash flow. They can help you see if your gym is making enough from its services compared to what you are paying the coaches to perform the service. Accounting will show you trends in your expenses. Seeing bad trends makes you aware of spending habits that need to be adjusted. Using accounting as the tool it should be will help you experience financial awareness worthy of your noble purpose.

"I (or my spouse) can do my own accounting." Software such as QuickBooks make accounting so easy to do. If they are using QuickBooks, a gym owner doesn't need to know about debits and credits and T accounts, or understand if assets increase with a debit or a credit, or how the Balance Sheet is connected to and affects the

---

[2] *Change Your Brain Change Your Life* by Daniel G Amen, MD; *The Willpower Instinct* by Kelly McGonigal, PhD; *Willpower Doesn't Work* by Benjamin Hardy

Profit and Loss statement. Because software makes bookkeeping easy, you can develop the skills to do your own accounting. Your members don't really need to go to your gym to get fit. They can do it at home. However, you know that those members get a more efficient workout at your gym than they could coming up with their own thing at home. They also free up time spent trying to decide what they should do, because at your gym they can just show up and follow directions.

I believe your time is better spent focused on higher-value activities rather than on your day-to-day bookkeeping. You can do all the coaching yourself, too, but most microgym owners know they need to let other coaches take over in order to grow a sustainable business. Further, I've found that gym owners who "can" do it themselves don't do the accounting regularly enough to get any use out of it. It is the task that is most often set aside for higher-value activities. During tax season, I let our microgym clients know we can get started on their tax returns as soon as they get us their financials. Almost all of them tell me they need a couple weeks to get the data to me because they "got behind" on keeping their books up to date. If this situation seems familiar to you, I strongly recommend getting this task off your plate.

"Accounting doesn't make sense." If "I can do my own accounting" is one side of a coin, the other side is "accounting doesn't make sense." This is just an excuse to give up on trying to learn anything about it. That attitude will get in the way of any and all benefits you can receive from having a good accounting system. I've only done one muscle-up in my life. They just don't make sense to me. Then again, neither did linking pull-ups or double unders, but now I can do both because I had proper guidance and instruction as I progressed and put effort into them. You *can* learn enough about accounting so that it makes sense to you.

"I just need to do enough accounting so I can file my taxes." If you believe this paradigm, you probably only update your accounting once a year. Do you remember every dollar you spent last week? Unless you didn't leave your house, chances are you can't. How are you going to remember what you spent eleven or twelve months ago? You do yourself a disservice when you only focus on accounting

for tax purposes. For one thing, as tax geniuses, we know from experience that you end up leaving tax deductions on the table. They are completely missed. Office supplies, missed internet deductions, travel, and auto expenses are some common ones. Missing deductions means you overpay on taxes. Also, you can make better decisions if the numbers are available for you more often.

"I don't need accounting. I'll just look at my bank balances." The Profit First system does leverage this behavior so that you could just look at your bank balances and get a feel for things. That being said, a better paradigm is: "I *do* need accounting and I can just look at my bank balances." With Profit First in place in your business, you will be able to look at your bank balances to help you make decisions. Without it, looking at bank balances leads to lots of overdraft charges. It can also give you a false sense of security when you see a high balance and forget about the checks you wrote that haven't been cashed yet or that you have some large expenses coming up soon. After learning the methods in this book, you will look at your bank balances with confidence.

THE "HOW MUCH MONEY DO YOU NEED TO BE HAPPY?" PARADIGM

Humans from time to time have found themselves chasing the holy grail of "more money." I, for one, have no problem with that quest. What I don't like is that, sometimes, those on the quest don't actually know why they are working so hard for "more money." More money for what purpose? Many would say, "to have more happiness." The idea that more money automatically means more happiness is a paradigm, and to give us the best chance at truly finding happiness, we need to rewrite this story.

More money equals more happiness has been a paradigm for so long that many have researched the question: "How much money is enough money?" "What is the magic number?" While there are a lot of studies we could look at, we are only going to highlight three. (One of the studies we aren't looking at said the happiness number was

$100 million. They were actually serious!) I'd like you to bear with me as we quickly review these three supposedly super-conclusive studies. I could jump straight to the punchline, but it won't land as well unless you have some of this data first.

2017 GALLUP POLL

In 2017, Gallup surveyed more than 1.7 million individuals from 164 countries. Andrew Jebb, a doctoral student at Purdue University, did research on the survey results.

What did they analyze? How much money makes individuals around the world happy?

The Conclusion: Andrew Jebb concluded that $95,000 is the magic number.

2017 GALLUP POLL—AGAIN?

USA Today had its own report using the same Gallup data Andrew Jebb analyzed.

What did they analyze? How much money makes individuals around the world happy? (The same question Andrew Jebb asked.)

The Conclusion: The magic number was $105,000.

2017 GALLUP POLL—A THIRD TIME?

Money.com reported its own findings yet again using the same Gallup data Andrew Jebb analyzed.

What did they analyze? How much money makes individuals around the world happy? (Exact same question as the other two. *Exact. Same. Question.*)

The Conclusion: The happiness number was between $60 and $75k.

Am I the only one who finds this hilarious? It's the same set of data, and Andrew Jebb, *USA Today*, and Money.com all came up with a different happiness number. The *same data*. Really conclusive findings, right?

If we can learn anything from these studies, it's that no one agrees on the same number, even when looking at the same data. Why is that? The real magic amount that you need to earn in order to be happy is not going to come from surveys and research. No one really knows how much money you personally need to be happy. You are the only one who can answer that question.

Have you heard a statement like this before? "If you have a problem and you have enough money to take care of it, then it's not really a problem." Someone who has problems is likely to not be happy. Solving them, then, can generally lead to increased happiness. While that could be true, the issue is that it still focuses on the idea that you need money to be happy—and not just any amount of money, enough money to throw at your problems. Again, it's this idea that there is a magic income number that makes you happy, and you can only be happy if you hit that number.

From 2001 to 2003, I lived in Argentina and I met some people who had very little based on any financial measure. Some of these people had two hundred-square-foot homes made out of twigs and mud. Others had slightly larger homes made of trees held up by stilts on the side of a mountain. Yet they were always smiling. The people I met never complained about some of the trivial things we often refer to as "First World Problems." They were some of the happiest people I've ever met, even though they had problems they couldn't throw money at to fix, even though their income was below what we call the poverty line in the United States.

Think about the following absurdity. "Man, this year I only made $74,999. I'm so friggin' miserable. My life is terrible." Fast forward to next year: "I made $75,000 this year. I've never been happier in my life." To some degree, the researchers are suggesting that the one-dollar difference makes life miserable or happy. Ridiculous.

We have to rewrite this paradigm. There is no magic number. I'm not trying to beat down on the guys who put the time together to analyze the data. I love numbers and what they reveal. However, our answers can only be as good as the questions we ask. The question they asked, "How much money makes individuals around the world happy?" was flawed. The real question needs to be "What do *I* need to be happy?" No researcher is ever going to be able to answer that question for you. Similar to how the Profit First methodology challenges the idea of only focusing on your overall Total Revenue, I ask you to challenge the idea that happiness is tied to a dollar figure. It's not the amount of revenue that is important; it's the way you show up in the world. It's the way you fulfill your noble purpose. It's the amount of what's left over which allows you to continue your legacy.

Let me tell you about two microgyms we work with. Multigym, LLC. is in a major US city. At the time of this example, the two owners had four locations earning more than a million dollars in revenue. Singlegym, LLC. is in a small market. They have one location and one owner. Their Total Revenue was $548,000. Which gym would you prefer to own? Bigger is better, right? Based on that philosophy, everyone would prefer to be Multigym, enjoying the million dollars in revenue.

Obviously, this is a setup. Is revenue the most important goal for gyms or any business? Is bigger always better? No and no. In order for a microgym to be relevant and sustainable, the cash left from revenue after paying expenses (*your profit*) is the most important. Multigym, LLC. had a net income of just over $90,000. That is just over 8% of their million dollar revenue. Singlegym, LLC, with its $548,000 in revenue, had a net income of just under $90,000. That's 16% of Total Revenue.

Now, with that additional info, which gym would you prefer to own? Manage four locations or just one to get the same result? Less work for same pay seems like the winner to me. Focusing on the size of the top line or number of locations is like asking generically how much money individuals need to be happy. What we need to do is focus on how much money we specifically need for our own personal needs because that is what we can control.

Some have argued that Multigym is serving more people and changing more lives than Singlegym, which fits the noble purpose of a microgym owner. The owners should be willing to work harder for the same pay as someone who works less because they are changing more lives. But how long can that last? If nothing changes and Multigym and Singlegym continue on their current paths, the owners of Multigym are much more likely to close shop and experience burnout, while Singlegym could be around for decades.

Obviously, I'm not using the real gym names of our clients in this example. The reality is that Singlegym had been working with us longer , which means they had been focused on profitability longer than Multigym. After a year of working with us and focusing on Profit First, Multigym was able to add a fifth location and purchase investment properties, while increasing their net income to 16% in three of their locations and 10% in the others. I know an 8% jump doesn't always sound sexy, but on a million dollars, that is an $80,000 increase. Focusing on profitability is a better indicator of how healthy your business is than focusing on the Total Revenue. It's also a better indicator of the probability the gym will be around to change the health of humanity. A healthy business will always be of better service to your members and to yourself than just being a big business ever would.

Your happiness is *your* emotion. You control it. I like how Mike said it in *Profit First*: "Wealth is a game of emotion. Business success is a game of emotion. Profit First is a game of emotion. It all comes down to the story we tell ourselves about what we're doing. "'Is what I'm doing making me happy or not?'"

You get a new car. You love it. After some time, your new car becomes second nature to you. It's now an expectation. It's not that you start hating your car; you just don't appreciate it the way you used to because now it is not a new car. It's just *your* car. What happens next? You want a new car. We like the emotion sparked by having a new car more than we like the lack of emotion from having the same ole' car. This doesn't just apply to cars, either. You can buy anything in this world with money, right? Often, we want to use our money to give us positive emotions. It's most human's tendency that, as their income increases, so does their lifestyle spending because they think they found the holy grail. The joke is if you ask most people the question, "How much money do you need to be happy?" their answer is, "Twice as much as I currently have."

The researchers tried to find an income number at which, if you made that amount of money, you would stop increasing your spending because you already have everything you need to be happy.

For most of us, discovering our own definition of happiness is a paradigm shift. We grind and wake up early to open the gym. We use any hour that doesn't have a class to squeeze in the million other things it seems we need to do. We then stay late for our evening classes or to clean up the gym after the final session. Then we try to juggle the main day-to-day tasks and never-ending daily fires. Because we don't think to stop for a second, we just keep going and subconsciously accept the crap the world tells us we need to be happy: More revenue is the only way. More clients is the only way. Get a bigger space. Maybe keeping a smaller space, limiting the number of members, and focusing on your profitability is all you need.

The holy grail isn't more money. The holy grail is finding true happiness. Don't let anyone else define your happiness for you. And that means, we each need to be responsible for discovering what happiness means to us individually.

THE PROFIT FIRST FLIP

Now let's review the ultimate paradigm related to finances and accounting. To understand it, we are going to take the next three hundred pages of this book to explore the history and origin of this paradigm. Punch me in the left nostril. That would be terrible, and I would never do that to you. So let me just give you a very short summary of the history.

According to historians, thousands of years ago, accounting systems were used in locations like Mesopotamia and Egypt. In fact, accounting is credited for helping early developments in writing, counting, and money. Five hundred years ago, a friar named Luca Pacioli published the very first accounting book using the "double-entry" method, which is the method still used today.

So, for a thousand years, the world has followed the same rules about accounting. It wasn't until 2008 when author Mike Michalowicz suggested in his first book, *The Toilet Paper Entrepreneur*, that he was using a different method that worked better.

While there are thousands of pages explaining the nuances of the old method, for the sake of summary and simplicity, we define the old method as this:

$$SALES - EXPENSES = PROFIT$$

That formula should sound and seem familiar. After all, it is in our DNA after thousands of years of our ancestors being exposed to it. The problem with this formula is that profit becomes the afterthought, what is left over, as if we have zero control over how much profit we generate. It shouldn't be that way.

What you are about to read is designed to blow your mind. It is also so simple that it may not blow your mind. However, by the end of the book, you will at least appreciate the subtle, sultry truth of this foundational concept. It's a little thing we like to call the Profit First Flip, and it looks like this:

$$SALES - \textbf{PROFIT} = EXPENSES$$

Notice that, mathematically, the formula hasn't changed. We are just changing our focus. You go into business to serve others and the idea of making a profit is the last thing on your mind. (Sometimes, it doesn't even make the list of priorities.) However, generating profit is a *must* in order for your gym to be sustainable. Hard work can only get you so far. On the other hand, hard work *plus* profit can take you to the finish line.

With the Profit First Flip, profit no longer is an afterthought or a happy accident. It is a conscious decision. You will determine the amount of profit you want to generate, and then use remaining revenue to run your gym. You have now created your profit first. Boom! You are now profitable.

If you've been chasing profitability for any length of time, I can appreciate it may be hard to believe profitability is this simple. This method of setting aside money for profit really works. As you dig into the financial workouts after each chapter, you will come to learn this for yourself.

Because you have made a conscious decision to be profitable does not mean past consequences like unpaid bills, excessive debt, or maxed-out credit cards automatically disappear. Because you are now profitable, though, you have given yourself the ability to do something about them. An overweight client can start eating healthy today, just as you can start "eating healthy" financially today by choosing to take your profit first. That overweight client is not going to wake up the next morning with 10 percent body fat, just as your gym won't be able to shed all the financial fat in just one night. *Profit First for Microgyms* puts you on the path to get a financially fit physique.

THE PROFIT PYRAMID

Have you ever heard of your reticular activator? Since we aren't really on the subject. I never enjoyed biology, so I don't want to go into scientific definitions, but your reticular activator controls your overall level of consciousness, as in, what you aware of in your environments.

I remember the first time I could afford a decent car. At that time, it was the largest financial commitment I had ever made. My goal was to not have buyer's remorse, so I studied the crap out of the cars in my price range. I came across the Infiniti G35x. I am pretty sure I had never seen an Infiniti. I was not even familiar with the brand, and yet, once I become aware of the G35x, and especially once it made it on my short list of possible cars to buy, I started seeing Infiniti's all over the place. Where did all of these Infiniti's come from? This phenomenon is thanks to my reticular activator. It raised my level of consciousness about the car I planned to buy.

What does this have to do with accounting and profitability? Well, let me tell you. By doing the Profit First Flip and setting up a predetermined amount of profit, which then forces you to use the remaining amount on expenses, your reticular activator will raise your level of consciousness—your level of awareness—about the areas that are helping your profit and the areas that are hurting your profit.

This book will walk you through each level of the Profit First Pyramid. The Profit First Flip is the foundational base. It challenges

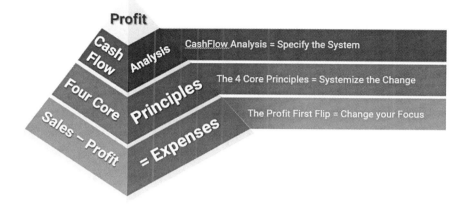

Profit

CashFlow Analysis = Specify the System

The 4 Core Principles = Systemize the Change

The Profit First Flip = Change your Focus

Cash Flow Analysis

Four Core Principles

Sales – Profit = Expenses

an ancient paradigm that no longer serves you. Rewriting the story and accepting the new formula to take profit first by using SALES – PROFIT = EXPENSES influences each level of the pyramid as you move up.

In Chapters 4–7, I'll explain the next level of the pyramid as I provide you with thorough instructions on the four core principles that make up the Profit First system. You will learn the essential elements that will help you focus on profit first, rather than expenses first, or even sales first. The four core principles will focus your financial efforts on profitability. Profitability will never again be an accident, but a conscious decision.

With the four core principles under your belt, you are then going to learn how to specifically apply them to your gym through a Cash Flow Analysis. This allows you to prescribe the correct financial actions your gym and members need you to take.

Each level of the pyramid leads to the capstone we lovingly refer to as *profit*. This is the equivalent of having one of your members combine your amazing workouts with proper nutrition. As they take action with your advice, they can't help but experience an increase in health.

When you have more profit, you ensure that you can focus on your noble motivations. If you have profit, you have uncountable options. If you don't have profit, your only option is to find it.

As Mike explains in *Profit First*, "The Profit First system was created because there appeared to be a gap for many business owners regarding the difference between making money (income) and taking money (profit)." The Profit First system and the Profit First Pyramid bridge that gap.

Mike further explains that making money and keeping some of it are just two activities to learn about cash flow. When describing his own story he said, "I had learned how to collect money, for sure, but I had never learned how to keep it, how to control it or how to grow it." Notice there are four things we should learn how to do relating to our cash.

1. How to collect cash
2. How to keep cash
3. How to control cash
4. How to grow cash

Monroe Miller, owner of Verity Speed & Strength, learned these things. However, he definitely didn't know all of them when he opened his gym in 2013. Before working on the Profit First Pyramid, he often thought he would have to close the gym because there was not enough cash to keep it going. "The gym wasn't growing, and our expenses were." This is not a great combination. As many do, he got into gym ownership because he thought he could do a better job running a business than the owner of the gym where he coached. He multiplied $150 per month by one hundred members and imagined himself swimming in a pool of cash.

Instead, Monroe ended up with a gym with stagnant membership and increasing expenses. In an attempt to grow revenue, he signed up with a gym marketing company. His monthly revenue tripled. Monroe added sixty new members in the span of two months.

He told me, "I thought that this is the new norm. I was making so much cash I wasn't paying attention to where any of it was going." In other words, he was collecting and growing cash, but what about keeping and controlling it? Since he was focused on the old paradigm of SALES - PROFIT = EXPENSES, the gym's expenses ended up quadrupling.

"And then the leads stopped," Monroe told me. Unfortunately, expenses don't stop at the same speed as revenue. It wasn't until he hired a coach that he realized the size of the hole he had put himself in. He started to climb the Profit Pyramid. Starting with the foundational Profit First flip, incorporating the four core principles, and then doing a Cash Flow Analysis on his gym, he integrated the Profit First system into every aspect of the gym's finances: collecting, keeping, controlling, and growing cash.

Monroe said, "Profit First is incredible. I have a plan and I'm no longer finding ways to spend money but finding ways to save money and grow the business. I feel in control. I'm making a profit. I'm paying myself and not blowing money. I finally believe I have a team that is guiding me on the financial side of my business where I was clearly struggling and I have so much hope for the future of my business."

FINANCIAL WORKOUT

Define what you really need in your life to experience happiness. What do your days look like? What activities are you doing, or not doing anymore? What time commitments maximize your happiness? Please do not think about what others would say or think about your answers. It's just you and your happiness you want to consider.

This exercise is going to be liberating for you. Remember the story of Étienne from the first chapter? You may find, as he did, that knowing what happiness looks like for you empowers you to say no to things that are really just distractions. Later in the book we will talk about paying yourself what you are worth. The exercises we give you there will go more smoothly if you take the time now to figure out what makes you happy.

CHAPTER 3

THE CORE PRINCIPLES OF PROFIT FIRST

Y OU NOW KNOW—OR REMEMBER—THAT THE STORIES WE TELL ourselves and the paradigms we currently believe can all be changed. If we judge ourselves and our own satisfaction levels with our lives, we may realize that we want a different story than what we are currently experiencing: a story with more happiness, more sustainability in our business, more freedom and flexibility in our average day. Perhaps you recognize that you've told yourself some of those stories that are holding you back. And now you recognize you can change it. Please realize that doing the same things you've done that got you to this point cannot be the same things you do to get you to a new and better point.

The Profit First Flip, SALES – PROFIT = EXPENSES, is one of these new paradigms we need to internalize. It's possible the story we tell ourselves about profit needs to change. You deserve to be profitable. Profit doesn't corrupt our noble motivation; it enhances and sustains it. A way to start changing the story is to first change our definition of profit. Mike defined it this way, "Our definition of profit is simple: cash in the bank, Cold. Hard. Cash. For us."

With Profit First, we aren't trying to swing for the fences here and hit homeruns. This is not a get rich quick scheme. It *is* a get "profit" quick scheme, but it isn't one of those high pressure, car salesman, selling snake oil, but wait there's more, you're getting in on the ground floor wasting your time and undeserving of your attention schemes.

My tax and accounting firm Incite Tax focuses on helping our clients create and grow their wealth. No matter what we are doing, we ask ourselves, "does this help our clients grow their wealth?"

One thing we have learned is that much of wealth creation is about consistency. It's about setting the goal to just "get on base." Singles, doubles, getting walked are all great ways to accomplish that.

It is super unlikely that a single event like a six-week challenge is going to take a failing gym to a profitable one. True growth in a microgym comes from client retention more than it comes from client acquisition, just as improving our profitability comes from smart, strategic, small moves and not a giant windfall of cash.

We would all love a windfall of cash and we also believe that, if said windfall of cash happened to us, we would be the exception and we would be able to use it to make our gym profitable. The reason the windfall of cash alone won't help us is because of the philosopher C. Northcote Parkinson and what is now called Parkinson's law.

PARKINSON'S LAW WAKE-UP CALL

I wasn't aware of Parkinson's law as a newly graduated controller (head accountant) at my first job out of college, but I still felt its negative effects.

I remember when the president of the company came running into my office, out of breath, and said, "John, you want to lock the door and not let anyone know you are here."

Being a controller is typically a dull, boring accounting position. So Doug's comment seemed a bit dramatic, especially since the company had just finished a record year with close to $30 million in revenue. We had just had our end-of-year celebration where we handed out bonus checks to our sales reps. They were large bonus checks: $10,000, $20,000, $30,000, a few were even larger than that.

I said, "Doug, Seriously, what gives?"

"Well," he replied, still out of breath—I guess he wasn't a member of your gym, "the owner didn't get that million-dollar loan he'd been working on, so all those checks we gave out last night are bouncing, and, if you recut any of the checks, those are going to bounce too."

Have you ever had one of those moments when you are talking to someone and what you hear them say sounds like the stupidest thing you have ever heard? It sounds so stupid your brain can't even comprehend the words that just came out of their mouth? That was this moment for me.

You must be thinking, "How does a company that does 30 million in revenue not have enough money to pay the sales reps?" You may also be wondering why I wouldn't know the answer to that question. After all, I was the head of the accounting department.

I did know the answer. In January of that year, in one of our executive meetings, I laid out a beautiful, gorgeous, super sexy spreadsheet for them. In the spreadsheet, I took the data from the previous year and showed them that for every sale the company made, the company kept eight dollars. That is a 1% margin, which, by the way, is really terrible.

In that meeting, I said, "Guys, there is this innovative, fresh idea that is sweeping the small business community, and I think implementing this idea here will make a huge difference. It's called a budget."

"John, you are so paranoid. We don't need a budget. We'll just sell more."

So when Doug entered my office in dramatic fashion, telling me checks were bouncing and I needed to lock the doors, the only thing I could respond with was, "Do you believe me now that we need a budget?"

It was the least satisfying "I told you so" moment of my life, because I was likely out of a job, along with a whole bunch of other employees. With paychecks bouncing and sales reps not getting paid, the company did, in fact, implode.

So how does a company that does $30 million in revenue declare bankruptcy in the same year? Enter Parkinson's law. It is always at work, even if you aren't aware of it.

Parkinson's law states that a resource expands to match the supply. Mike explained it in *Profit First*, " The demand for something expands to match its supply. You see the more we have of something, the more of it we consume." In the case of my employer, the expenses expanded to match the cash available to spend. The more revenue we had, the more we spent.

I haven't met a micro gym owner who is doing $30 million in revenue. However, after more than ten years helping people deal with their money, I have seen Parkinson's law at work in gym's with annual income as small as $25,000.

Luckily, Profit First is kryptonite against Parkinson's law. It says, "Okay, Mr. Parkinson. I see your law. I'm not going to deny it exists, but I'm going to put boundaries around the cash so that you can't rear your ugly head, jerk face."

TRADITIONAL ACCOUNTING HAS ITS PLACE

One last thing before we get to the core principles of Profit First. The ancient formula of SALES–EXPENSES=PROFIT still has a place in business. But as Mike explains in his book, "It was never intended to manage only cash. It is part of a system for understanding all the elements of your business. The system has three key reports: the income statement, the cash flow statement, and the balance sheet. There is no question that you need to understand these reports (or work with [Incite Tax] because [we] do), because the reports will give you a holistic view of your company; they are powerful and highly useful tools. But the essence of SALES–EXPENSES=PROFIT is horribly flawed.

Ideally, you would follow all the accounting instructions necessary to pinpoint your numbers. On a weekly basis, you would study your income statement, tie it into your balance sheet, and, of course, do an analysis of your cash flow. Next you would run the critical ratios and tie all this into your budget and projections. Then you would evaluate the associated KPIs (key performance indicators, such as average revenue per member). You would do it all and you would know exactly where your profits stood at any time. But you don't, do you?"

Why would you? You don't have time to run your business and run an accounting business because that's what it would take to have all that dialed in properly. This ancient formula was designed for accountants, which, no offense, (or maybe a compliment depending on how you view it) you probably aren't. As Mike states, " To successfully run a profitable business, we need a system that is designed for humans."

Hey, what a coincidence! The system you are about to learn is exactly that! Mike explained, "Profit First can instantly tell us the truth about the health of our business, one that we can look at and know instantly what we need to do to get healthy and stay healthy; Profit First tells us what we can actually spend and what needs to be reserved, and Profit First doesn't require us to change but automatically works with our natural behaviors."

THE PROFIT FIRST CORE PRINCIPLES

You are in for a treat because you have a microgym advantage that owners of other kinds of business do not have. You understand fitness, health, and losing weight better than any others. It just so happens that in *Profit First*, Mike uses the analogy of healthy eating to explain the Profit First core principles. This is like getting a head start.

You know what good nutrition means for the body. Nutrition is to your body as accounting and finances are to your business. If you are constantly putting crap in your body, exercise alone can only take your fitness so far. If you don't have an accounting and cash flow management system, lots of sales will only take your business so far. I just told you about the company that did almost 30 million dollars in revenue the same year it declared bankruptcy. They ignored the nutrition component for their business because they didn't respect accounting or good cash flow management. Profit First is like a nutritious daily serving of fruits and veggies for your gym.

With SALES – PROFIT = EXPENSES as the foundation for the Profit First system, the four core principles build on that foundational concept. These principles are:

1. Small Plates
2. Eat Veggies First
3. Remove Temptation
4. Eat Smaller Meals More Frequently (The 10/25 Rhythm)

Let's look at each of the four principles:

SMALL PLATES

Mike summarizes an important research study he learned about one night while watching PBS. His fingers may or may not have been covered in delicious Cheetos dust. He summarized, "In 2012, a report by Korert Van Ittersum and Brian Wansink in the Journal of Consumer Research concluded that the average plate size in America had grown 23 percent between the years 1900 and 2012, from 9.6 inches to 11.8 inches. Running the math, the article explains that should this increase in plate size encourage an individual to consume just fifty more calories per day, that person would put on an extra five pounds of weight each year. Year after year, that adds up to a very chunky monkey." And that, we know, makes doing burpees, pull-ups, and all workouts that much harder.

Enter the smaller plates core principle. Studies show that if people want to lose weight, an easy trick is to simply use a smaller plate. Since we are trained to eat everything on our plate, we will still feel satisfied. We consume fewer calories because there isn't room for the second scoop of delicious, fluffy, creamy garlic mashed potatoes.

EAT VEGGIES FIRST

I've been fighting this data internally and emotionally for a while. Some people apparently believe that, if you eat your vegetables before you get to the meat and potatoes and Reese's peanut butter cups, you have less room for those less healthy to completely unhealthy food choices.

REMOVE TEMPTATION

If I were an alcoholic it would be pretty silly for me to hang out at a bar. As a sugarholic, stocking sugary, delicious, Double Stuf Oreos is a terrible idea. (Have you seen The Most Stuf Oreos? Friggin' genius.)

"Honey do you want one?"

"Yes, please."

My wife hands me one, and I'm like, "I said I wanted one… as in one sleeve. What did you think I meant when I said I'd have one?"

This core principle is about *not* putting yourself in a position to be tempted in the first place. So in the case of Oreos, I really shouldn't bring them into the house.

EAT SMALLER MEALS MORE FREQUENTLY (THE 10/25 RHYTHM)

Let's think about the bear versus the horse. A bear hibernates and then eats large and less frequent meals. The horse grazes. Comparing the two animals, while the bear is powerful, the bear is also large and round. The horse, on the other hand, is shredded!

Eating smaller meals more frequently helps people lose weight and stay trim. For businesses, we might occasionally come across the scenario in which the gym owner doesn't touch their accounting all year. Come tax time, which is usually sixteen months or more after the fact, they finally sit down to look at the entire previous year. Sitting down to consume an entire years' worth of accounting is the same thing as eating like a bear. We'd rather be shredded like the horse.

The four core principles of Profit First are based on dieting principles. This book will show you how these dieting principles create sound cash flow behavior. In reality, these four core principles are actually giving us a system and framework in which we will build our profit focus.

The Profit First system will have multiple bank accounts (smaller plates). It will give you the order and priority of allocating your money into these different bank accounts (eating veggies first). It will put protections in place so you don't touch the money you are setting aside for specific purposes (removing temptations), and it will schedule when to do the allocations (smaller meals more frequently).

These four simple core principles are the foundation of the most successful business cash flow management system you are ever going to come across. Profit First trains you to take *your* profit *first*, instead of letting expenses just happen. You know as well as I do that getting and staying fit is all about our choices. In this book, you'll learn how to ensure that profit becomes a deliberate decision, *your decision,* rather than something you hope will happen one day.

A REAL-LIFE PROFIT FIRST MIRACLE

When you make the decision to be profitable, you may have a similar story to Jason Fernandez, owner of CrossFit Rife. Before starting Profit First, the most Jason had ever paid himself in a given year was about $12,000. He was treating the gym as supplemental income, which was a mindset that lead him to mediocre results. Before Profit First, tax season was stressful. He never felt prepared for it. He dreaded what he was going to owe because he wasn't sure how much it would be or how he was going to pay it.

Jason's mindset before Profit First was to run the business based on upcoming income and not the cash on hand. Basically, he was spending money he didn't have yet. He remembers times that he wrote and sent out checks not knowing if they would clear, and his microgym ran at a loss for five consecutive years.

After he implemented Profit First, his business did a one-eighty. Now he had new problems and challenges: better challenges, such as trying to figure out what to spend their money on instead of wondering if they were going to have money to spend at all. CrossFit Rife went from a 0% to 10% net income in less than a year. His OWNER'S PAY quintupled, and they now have dedicated budgets for equipment, continuing education, marketing, and taxes. What once was one of the biggest stresses about tax season is now comfortable because he can pay taxes when they are due.

CrossFit Rife is now a healthy business that is more prepared to serve its members. Jason's mindset is completely different. He told me, "We have been able to create a healthy business that is sustainable while providing an ever-improving product that allows us to over-deliver to people that walk in our doors."

He explained that it wasn't as if they didn't have enough revenue before; they just didn't know what to *do* with the revenue. Now they do. That confidence makes the future very bright and exciting.

Needless to say, Jason is a big fan of Profit First. He says, "If a gym owner wants to relieve themselves of the financial stresses of operating a business, Profit First will help them get their revenue organized and accounted for. It only improves your service to your clients and creates a business that serves you, so you aren't a slave to the thing you love."

You may be thinking that is all good and well for Jason. But you may still have a concern that, if you set aside your profits, how are you going to grow?

Mike answers that in *Profit First*, "This is a question that gets asked a lot. By now, hopefully you are convinced that chasing growth for its own sake is how you wind up broke and out of business. But that doesn't mean growth doesn't matter, or that you shouldn't want it. Growth strategies can be great. A common misconception though is that you can only have one or the other, as though it's an either-or proposition. Either you could grow or you could be profitable—you surely couldn't do both. Wrong. What we've found is that the fastest, healthiest growth comes from businesses that prioritize profit. And it is not because they plow money back into their businesses. Businesses that plow back their profits aren't truly profitable; they are just holding money temporarily (feigning profit), then spending it just like any other expense. Profit First sparks faster growth because it makes you reverse engineer your profitability. When you take your profit first, your business will tell you immediately whether it can afford the expenses you are incurring; it will tell you whether you are streamlined enough; it will tell you whether you have the right margins. If you find that you can't pay your bills after taking profit first, you must address all those points and make the fixes."

It doesn't matter where you are starting from because the Profit First system will take you where you want to go. Maybe you can relate to Jason and his low take-home pay. Profit First gave him the focus and direction he needed just as it can give you more focus and direction. You, too, could experience the faster growth Profit First stimulates.

FINANCIAL WORKOUT

As you get into the details of the four core principles in the upcoming chapters, your financial workouts will take you down the path of getting Profit First officially set up in your gym. I'm also going to walk you through the process of analyzing the financial health of your business. If your accounting system is accurate, the analysis will give you the best results.

For this financial workout, sit down with your bookkeeper and confirm that your accounting records are accurate. Make sure your transactions are being categorized consistently to the same categories. For example, make sure Zen Planner is always booked under Dues and Subscriptions, not Computer and Internet one month and then Dues and Subscriptions the next month. Make sure that your bank accounts and credit card accounts are reconciled. Also make sure all your business bank accounts and credit card accounts are actually entered into your accounting software. You should do this anyway just because you are a responsible gym owner, but this will also get your accounting ready for the Cash Flow Analysis you are about to learn.

CHAPTER 4

PRINCIPLE ONE—
SMALLER PLATES

CORE PRINCIPLES AND ANALOGIES ARE GREAT. TAKING DIETING principles and applying them to accounting is also great. What's not great is the perpetual marketing piece. You take the time to read a really long email or watch a video because the subject line resonates with you, only to get through it to realize the professional didn't tell you a damn thing, not one solid piece of anything worth hearing because what they are saying is just hype crap. It gets you excited since they use every cliché one liner they can think of. It's like going to one of those rah-rah seminars where the goal is to get you so emotionally high that the logical part of your brain is silenced.

If you ever read *Profit First* by Mike Michalowicz or any of his other books, you will know that Mike is big on application. So he gives lots of action items that, if followed, can help business owners make positive change. When he agreed to let me write this book, he made sure to emphasize that I better provide real life application for you, the microgym owner, or he was going to rip my arms off, beat me with them, then marinate them and cook them on his smoker. (Okay, he didn't really say it that way. But you get the picture.) So how do these diet analogies translate to your Profit First cash flow management system?

Small plates help people lose weight. That is, if you believe studies that have conclusive evidence, which I do. Most microgyms have one bank account. I want you to think of that one bank account as a large plate. With one large plate, you are ~~begging~~ asking for Parkinson's law to destroy you. Remember, resources expand to meet the supply. With one and only one bank account, your expenses will expand to meet the cash available to spend. With all that cash sitting on the one plate, we can't help but spend it. And that leaves you wondering how to pay yourself, where is the cash to pay your taxes, and how are you going to make payroll.

The Profit First cash flow management system requires you to create other smaller bank accounts. Each account has a specific purpose, which will be covered in detail later. For now, just know you'll create multiple bank accounts for quarterly PROFIT distributions, OWNER'S PAY, TAXES, future EQUIPMENT, INCOME, and some other possibilities.

Eating veggies first helps our bodies feel full before we convince ourselves we still have room for that delicious breath mint pie with its crust of crushed Mint Oreos baked in butter and a layer of mint chocolate chip ice cream mixed with Junior Mints topped off with another layer of crushed Mint Oreos baked in butter. (Hypothetically speaking, that is.)

With this cash flow management system, the order in which you allocate your money is important. I explain why this is the order a microgym should follow in the next chapter. First, transfer cash to an account reserved for OWNER'S PAY, because an owner working in the business is the most important team member. Always make sure the most important team member is paid. Then, put money in the TAX account. The IRS sucks. No doubt. The government sucks at spending your money. Again, no doubt. But we do pay taxes sometimes. If you owe legitimate taxes, the smallest legal amount possible, you don't want to get behind on that bill. You don't want to willingly invite bullies into your backyard. So we set money aside for taxes. Then, put cash in the PROFIT account. Use the remaining funds for operating expenses and some of the other small plate accounts.

Removing temptation would involve not bringing that breath mint pie into the house in the first place or making sure anything Reese's is hidden from yours truly. If it is hard to find, it's easier to resist the temptation. From a cash flow management standpoint, your PROFIT account and your TAX account will build up a healthy cash balance. So in order to avoid the temptation of stealing from yourself, Profit First suggests moving these two accounts to a separate banking institution and setting it up so that those accounts are super inconvenient to access. Mike's "remove temptation" bank is a more than two-hour drive away. That particular institution also does not have online banking, and his account does not provide checks. The only way for him to get that money is to drive the two hours. That is truly removing the temptation.

Eating smaller meals more frequently allows the body to feel fuller throughout the day to avoid the swings of feeling overstuffed or being starved. Most people make terrible eating decisions when they are starving. With cash flow, you can't do anything about things you discover doing your accounting only once per year. Looks as though you had an unnecessary subscription all year. Looks as though your staff costs were too high a percentage of your revenue. You didn't realize how much was actually spent on advertising. (Nah. I'm sure that probably never happens.)

Now, what if you sat down twice a month: smaller meals and more frequent on, let's say, the 10th and the 25th. That is why we also call this principle the 10/25 rhythm. When you dig into your cash flow about every fifteen days, you won't let unnecessary expenses slide. This is the way to keep your microgym lean and trim.

Let's really dig into each principle starting with Smaller Plates.

SMALLER PLATES

People serve themselves in proportion to plate size. It doesn't matter how big the plate is, they will fill it up. The small plate study we referenced in the last chapter also found that people consume 92 percent of what they serve themselves, no matter how big the plate is.

Researchers gave the participants a ten-inch plate instead of the standard twelve-inch plate. People filled up the plate and consumed about 92 percent of what was on the plate. But they felt "satiated." They felt full. By using the smaller plate, they consumed 22 percent less calories.

The researchers believe this was related to a phenomenon known as the Delboeuf Illusion. Look at the two dots. Which one is smaller?

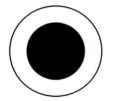

The black circles are the same size, but one appears smaller when it is placed inside a larger circle.

Think about how we currently use our bank accounts. We have one checking account. Maybe we also have an unused or barely used savings account, but usually it's just the one account that is the focus.

Now let's reflect on what the smaller plate study teaches us about human nature. We serve ourselves in proportion to the plate size and then we consume 92 percent of it. This means that we will keep using our bank account funds based on what is needed in the moment, often using around 92 percent of what is in there. This puts a business in the position of being paycheck to paycheck. If an expense needs to be paid, we sure hope there is income that will provide the cash needed to cover it. When you have one bank account, a good habit of planning out expenses, and saving cash for future expenses is likely a fantasy.

The smaller plate study also showed that even with a smaller portion of food, participants still felt full. The same thing will happen to you as you add "smaller plates" or, in this case, more bank accounts. As you follow the system, your business will still have sufficient cash to cover expenses, allowing it to feel "full."

Mike and I are not just asking you to set up bank accounts because we have a weird, multiple bank account fetish. (Hey! Stop it! We don't!) Each account will have a specific purpose, which will allow you to use the cash in that account for the purpose for which you set it aside in the first place. The best part is that you will still feel that your business is getting things done the way you want. In fact, you may feel this for the very first time.

This multiple bank account strategy is also the way to make sure you have a place to put what you should be paying yourself, your future profit distributions, your tax obligation, and the other things you identify for these smaller plate accounts.

What we are doing here is telling Mr. Parkinson to shove it. We reduce the plate size of our operating expenses. This allows us (not forces us) to spend differently. As Mike says in *Profit First*, "So rather than try to curb my spending habit, I would create the experience of having less cash on hand than I actually had, and then I would find ways to still make things work."

Let's go over the Essential Seven Accounts you'll need to set up:

INCOME ACCOUNT

The purpose of this account is to receive payments for the services you provide. It never writes a check. It receives member deposits and then transfers money into the other bank accounts. (We will cover how you know what amounts to transfer to each account in Chapter 8).

When Mike introduced Profit First, he did not originally have the INCOME account as one of the primary accounts a business owner should set up. But in his revised edition, he made it a mandatory account. I can tell you from experience I now understand why this has to be a mandatory account.

The entire first year I ran Profit First for Incite Tax, I did not have an INCOME account. Instead, my deposits were going directly into my operating expense (OPEX) account. But each time I made transfers into the other accounts, I seemed to be short. I never seemed to have enough cash to cover the bills that were due. I felt frustrated and, frankly, like a fraud, because there I was teaching others how to run the Profit First system and it wasn't really "working" for me.

Then, in a meeting for Mastery Level Profit First Professionals, Mike explained the purpose of the INCOME account and that, if he could do it again, he would include the INCOME account as a primary account and not an optional account. It was as if the heavens opened, and an angelic light shone down on Mike and he was speaking directly to me, "Nimrod, go set up an INCOME account, and the system will work for you."

I did, and it did. I wish I could tell you all the neuro- and psychological reasons that explain why that changed everything. I'm sure Parkinson's law has something to do with it. I just know from personal experience that the system doesn't work without an INCOME account. I lived the year without it and felt the frustration. Now I live with the INCOME account in place and I'm no longer frustrated. My bank balances continue to increase through each cycle, I have enough cash to pay my bills, and I don't have to freak out about where the money is going to come from when the tax man comes to take his pound of flesh.

TEAM MEMBER EXPENSE

Paying team members is one of the top two expenses for most microgyms. In our experience, we have found having a dedicated "plate" for this expense is the best practice. It's important to note that if you are coaching classes as the owner, the pay you should receive for coaching the class comes out of this account. Your other pay should come out of the OWNER'S PAY account, which we'll go over next. The reason we have your coaching pay come out of the TEAM MEMBER expense is that most gym owners are working toward stepping out of day-to-day coaching. They want the freedom to step into a class if they want to and not because they *have* to. With that goal in mind, paying for your own coaching work out of the TEAM MEMBER plate lets you see if you have the cash flow to replace yourself. Without this focus, the common behavior is that you end up coaching the class and not paying yourself for the work.

OWNER'S PAY

The purpose of this account is to hold money that belongs to the owners who work day-to-day in the gym. If you are coaching classes, that comes out of the TEAM MEMBER Expense. OWNER'S PAY is for all your other compensation. If you are doing janitorial services, handling social media posts or blogs, training other coaches, or anything else that is part of operations, you should be making a wage comparable to what the market pays for that type of work. I'm not an elitist and I try my hardest to never take myself too seriously, but there is a belief all of us microgym owners need to adopt: If we are working in the business, then we are the most important employee, and a good boss always makes sure the most important employee gets paid.

Having said that, some of our clients don't set up an OWNER'S PAY account because they just transfer the amount they earned from OWNER'S PAY directly into their personal account. In other words, their personal account is their "smaller plate" for OWNER'S PAY.

Look. Profit First is a set of guidelines to be adapted to your exact situation. So if you think just using your personal account for OWNER'S PAY is perfect for you, then proceed. I would like to provide three reasons though why you may consider having an OWNER'S PAY account, and they're based on my own experience using Profit First.

Reason 1: I have an OWNER'S PAY account for my tax business because tax season at the beginning of the year and extension season in October provide an influx of cash; the other months much less cash comes in. This makes my cash flow inconsistent month to month. An OWNER'S PAY account, can build up a reserve during the months when there is a ton of customer payments, which can then be tapped into during the months when customer payments are sparse at best. I know that many gyms have pretty consistent cash flow compared to my tax firm. But maybe it isn't as consistent as we think. One month you could sell a lot more personal training sessions (which means the member will have to eventually be resold on more PT sessions or on another service to keep their cash coming in) and another month there are no personal training sessions sold. Maybe you have competitions or events at your gym that bring in some nice additional revenue. Maybe you do apparel sells a few times a year instead of every month. It's possible you have members cancel in summer since they aren't in town but then rejoin during the school year. In Utah, members cancel during ski season because they want to spend every waking minute on the slopes and they don't want to run the risk of extra soreness from workouts ruining their ski runs. Having an OWNER'S PAY account helps you smooth out the inconsistent cash flow months.

Reason 2: I want to ensure (because I made my wife a promise) that I'm bringing home the same dollar amount each month. This allows my wife and I to have a predictable budget. Tax season gives me lots of deposits in my INCOME account and so my OWNER'S PAY account increases a lot during those months. However, May, July, November, December, and January are not as great. Sometimes, I haven't been able to make enough in those months to bring home the promised dollar amount. So my OWNER'S PAY account becomes a reserve for me that gets a surplus of cash in the fat months and can be depleted in the starvation months. The best part is, at the end of the year, anything left in that account gets transferred to my personal account because it is OWNER'S PAY that I earned.

Reason 3: In addition to working as a reserve account for me, it also protects me against Parkinson's law in my personal account. As my income increases in real life, we are living on the same amount of money we know we can comfortably live on, without the risk and temptation to increase the cost of our lifestyle.

PROFIT ACCOUNT

The purpose of this account is to provide a quarterly profit distribution to all owners of the gym. As an owner of the business, having equity in an investment, you need to earn a return on that investment (ROI, return on investment). If an investment isn't giving you a return, why would you keep it? Your microgym is worth keeping, so we need to make sure you get a return.

Again, the purpose of OWNER'S PAY is for the owners who work in the day-to-day of the business. If an owner doesn't work in the gym day-to-day, then they don't get any money from the OWNER'S PAY account. But when it comes to the PROFIT account, all owners get money from it.

What do you do with these quarterly profit distributions? Well, whatever the crap you want to do, except, plough the money back into your business. PROFIT is supposed to be pure celebration money. That being said, if you have debt, in Chapter 9 we will go over how the quarterly profit distribution can be used to pay down that debt faster.

I would also like to point out you will only be distributing 50% of the balance in your PROFIT Account each quarter. The remaining 50% stays in the account as a type of rainy day fund.

TAX ACCOUNT

The purpose of this account is to save money for your income tax burden. I specify income tax here because taxes like sales tax and payroll tax would be coming out of your operating expense (OPEX) account. The TAX account is just for income taxes. It would be very rare and would need very specific reasons, which we will cover in Chapter 10, that you would choose a C Corp for your tax structure. It's more likely, however, that you have what the tax system calls a "flow through" entity. It's called "flow-through" because the tax burden flows to your individual tax return. That means, technically, you are paying personal income tax on the income your gym generates. Instead of having you save money out of your OWNER'S PAY amount, we believe your gym should cover the tax burden on that income.

If you think about the OWNER'S PAY account, the amount you receive needs to be the amount you design your lifestyle around. That's your regular pay. We don't like the idea that you should then have to take out of your lifestyle funds the amount that you owe in taxes. That's why this account is part of the cash flow management system and why it's a required account.

EQUIPMENT ACCOUNT

This account is for the gym to buy new equipment or repair existing equipment. We know that your equipment will not last forever. Bikes and rowers need to be maintained. Weight plates fall apart. Clips and bands break. Yoga mats and ab mats get disgusting and start growing mold. You know this. So, we might as well prepare by giving ourselves an account for it.

Setting aside money in the EQUIPMENT account allows you to handle equipment emergencies *and* take advantage of equipment deals. Poorly functioning equipment isn't in your members best interest. Having a profitable gym grants you the ability to give your members a top-notch experience with well-functioning equipment.

OPERATING EXPENSE (OPEX) ACCOUNT

The purpose of this account is to pay the bills and expenses of operating your business. The good news is, you already have this account set up because we normally just use your existing bank account. This is the only account that you need actual checks for. This one is just that straightforward. Money in this account is what you use to operate the business.

LIMITED RESOURCES AND NASA

So why does this method of multiple bank accounts work? Here's Mike's answer, "When less money is available to run your [gym], you will find ways to get the same or better results with less. By taking your profit first, and moving money to these other accounts first, you will be forced to think smarter and innovate more."

Humans (which is basically anyone who doesn't work with the IRS) have shown that in situations with limited resources, they have accomplished amazing things. Apollo 13 was one of those situations. The movie tells the story better than I can. But in summary, their mission was to land on the moon, and an explosion in one of the oxygen tanks forced the crew to return to Earth as quickly as possible with no moon landing.

Losing one oxygen tank meant at some time before the shuttle made it back to earth, the astronauts would run out of oxygen. Since oxygen tends to be a big deal for us humans, they were going to need another air scrubber pronto. So the scientists at NASA grabbed all the parts the crew members would have access to in their space capsule and, using just those items, they were tasked with figuring out how to make one. Normally this process would take three months. The problem was that in three months, the crew members would be done-zo. With the limited resources on the shuttle, and with the limited resource of time, the scientists at NASA came up with a lifesaving solution in three hours.

The Apollo 13 story is so amazing it reminds me of Mike's amazing story about toothpaste. How do normal people use toothpaste? When you get a new tube, resources are abundant, so you use ample amounts. "I'll lay it on thick," you think. "Oh crap, the paste fell off the brush right into the sink. Oh well, I'll just put on another ginormous dollop, no big deal."

But what happens when you get to the end of the tube? The tube is getting really flat, and squeezing out more toothpaste becomes a hand and forearm workout. What happens now if the paste falls into the sink? You start racking your brain trying to remember the last time you cleaned the sink. If you are like me, you might not be able to recall that, so you convince yourself the sink is clean and scoop that fallen toothpaste onto your brush.

You certainly aren't using Hershey kiss-sized dollops anymore. How much is enough? So you read the instructions and see it says apply a one-inch strip to your toothbrush. Well, how thin can that one-inch strip be?

Then there are the many ways we get every last atom out of the tube of toothpaste. You roll from the bottom; maybe you use a rubber band, so the bottom won't roll back. Or maybe you buy a tube squeezer product. (I'm not kidding. There is an actual product called EZ Squeeze Tube Squeezer designed to help with this issue.) Or maybe you cut off the end with scissors and squeeze the rest out of the bottom. My favorite is to just suck the toothpaste directly into my mouth. The point is that there are lots of creative methods people have come up with for getting toothpaste out of the tube.

What do Apollo 13 and toothpaste teach us? When resources are limited, we have proven to be capable of making them work for our needs. I know you have heard the stories (and maybe you are one of these stories) where the microgym owner started in a garage, or they had fifty square feet of someone else's space, or they just had a small three-hundred-square-foot shack to use, but they made it work. Chris Cooper, founder of Two Brain Business, told me his first space was so small that, as his membership grew, he would have one-on-one sessions on the landing of the stairs. You just make it work.

As I mentioned earlier, when I was working with just the one bank account, with the same human nature and tendencies as most other business owners, things were a struggle. December and January can be really slow collection months for a tax business. I was super stressed hoping I'd make enough just to cover our personal bills. I felt as though my business was almost a Ponzi scheme. I had to use the current, right-now income to cover payroll from last month. I had to utilize my ninja skills with tax strategies to make sure I didn't owe a lot, because I didn't have the cash to pay any taxes. As the business grew, I knew I needed more help, but I was never sure if I would be able to afford it. After all, it didn't seem I could cover my existing bills and payroll. I was working tons of hours: eighty- to one-hundred-hour weeks during tax season, sixty hours outside of tax season. I think my hourly rate was around ten dollars an hour at one point. Super sucky for sure!

Then Profit First came into my life. Even though the first year wasn't as great as it could have been because I wasn't using a separate INCOME account, it was still better than working with just one bank account for everything. How about two years later? Forget about it! All those pain points and struggles I had are now strengths. My take-home pay is reliable, and I can comfortably make that transfer every month. I use this month's income to cover this month's expenses. My TAX account is used to pay my tax burden. That in itself is a raise, because I was relying on my take-home pay to cover taxes in the past. It's much easier for me to figure out if we can afford more staff now that I have a clear picture of our cash flow trends. I also enjoy quarterly profit distributions. Well, my wife enjoys them, at least. It seems she has a never-ending list of things she wants to do around the house. My backyard has basically become a record of what I've done with my profit distributions, which is just fine by me.

Profit First for Microgyms works. Having multiple bank accounts works. That being said, let me mention a common pushback we get regarding multiple bank accounts. Some gym owners believe, and use as an excuse to not start this method, that this is going to complicate the hell out of their accounting.

And here is my long-winded response to that pushback: nope, not true. Yes, this system adds more bank accounts. Yes, those accounts need to be tracked. But these accounts are only adding a few transactions each month. They are holding pens more than anything. It isn't that much more work and the extra clarity is what we owners need.

FINANCIAL WORKOUT

Your financial workout is to set up the necessary bank accounts. You'll keep your existing one and rename it your operating expense (OPEX) account. Then set up accounts for INCOME, TAX, PROFIT, EQUIPMENT, TEAM MEMBERS, and OWNER'S PAY.

You will need to instruct your merchant processor to switch the accounts they are using for credit card deposits from members. In my experience, all merchant processors have a simple one-page form to make this switch.

Some banks charge dumb fees, so make sure you check first to see if they will increase your bank fees because you want more accounts. There are friendly banks and credit unions that don't have fees for accounts that have just a few transactions. This is a foundational step to implementing Profit First in your gym. Mike would probably say something like, "Don't walk, *run*, to the bank to get these set up." But I know you were already planning on running anyway because you like working out.

[BONUS] BANKING TIPS

A tip I want to share about the banking process is that, as a gym owner, you really need a personal contact at the bank you use. All banks have employees that do this liaison work. I personally bank with Chase and it took me two attempts to find a contact who will stick. The first small business liaison at my branch never got back to me. So I went into another branch and found someone who responds to my emails and phone calls. Now I direct all my questions to this person's email instead of trying to figure out the answer from the website or playing a lengthy phone tree game.

A second banking tip is that, once you have that personal contact, setting up accounts becomes painless. You tell them you want to set up some more bank accounts and that you want them to have all the paperwork ready so that when you come in all you have to do is sign.

I had a client who flew me from Utah to California to consult with him for two days. You know what we ended up doing? We spent one of the days at the bank so he could set up all these accounts. What a waste of time! Your time is valuable. Don't waste it.

CHAPTER 5

EAT VEGGIES FIRST

A S I'M SAVORING EVER SO QUICKLY AND WITH LITTLE DISCIPLINE, a Cadbury egg, I'm reminded of the soundness of the principle: Eat veggies first. I couldn't find an awesome study like the smaller plate study to describe this concept. It's really not rocket science, though, is it? By eating your vegetables first, you fill up on healthy food, leaving you less desire (supposedly) to pig out on bad carbs or desserts. Or Cadbury eggs.

So what are the financial veggies you should be eating first? What's the actual application of this dieting principle to your Profit First system? (I love this principle because it's all about you!) The best thing your gym can do for you is give you money. First because you work hard and deserve it, and second because you cannot fulfill your noble purpose if you can't sustain your life and that takes cash. So paying yourself, getting cash for your benefit, that is a cash veggie. (And it tastes as sweet as a dessert, if you are into that type of thing.)

Remember, this cash flow management system is called Profit First. That means, the first thing you do, not the second thing you do, but the *first* thing you do is take your profit. Nothing comes before profit. But in reality, the word "profit" as used in the name of this system, means "cash for the benefit of the owner." After having taught this system to hundreds of microgym owners, a more descriptive title might have been Cash for the Benefit of the Owner First… but, darn it all, that doesn't sound as sexy as "Profit."

Let's look at your new bank accounts. Which ones are for your benefit?

OWNER'S PAY benefits you because that is compensation for working in the day-to-day, nitty gritty of the business. You need to be compensated for this work. And the intention is that you will be able to afford your lifestyle on this amount.

The **PROFIT** account benefits you because this represents the return on investment you get from owning your gym. The more profitable the gym, the bigger the "dividend" payment. Profit distributions are done at the end of each quarter and profit distributions go to all owners, including those who are not involved in the daily tasks and operations.

The **TAX** account benefits you because, with a profitable business, you will have a tax burden that needs to be covered. The gym is creating this tax burden for you; it's only fair that the gym also pay for the taxes. You should not have to take money out of your take-home pay or profit distributions to cover income tax. Most owners have to save for their taxes out of their take-home pay. Well, not anymore. And because of that, the **TAX** account is giving you a raise because the gym is now going to cover it for you.

You have three accounts that benefit you directly. **OWNER'S PAY**, **TAX**, and **PROFIT** And when you sit down twice a month to allocate the **INCOME** deposits into your multiple bank accounts (smaller plates), you will first allocate, in this order, **OWNER'S PAY**, **TAX**, and **PROFIT**. Then, you'll allocate to **EQUIPMENT** and **OPEX** (operating expenses). In Chapter 8, we will go over how much money you transfer into these accounts. For now, we are still establishing the foundational concepts of the system.

I know in *Profit First*, Mike says to allocate first to the **PROFIT** account. And I am asking you to allocate to your **OWNER'S PAY** account first. Why? I want to make sure you are paying yourself first because one of the first steps of knowing you deserve to be profitable is paying yourself a livable wage. Many gym owners aren't doing that. If you are not paying yourself a bare minimum livable wage, this is where you draw the line in the sand. That's why you need to first allocate to **OWNER'S PAY**.

Remember, this book could be called *Cash for the Benefit of the Owner First*. Of these cash veggie accounts, we have also found that when you are able to pay yourself consistently each month, you don't reach burnout. If you must choose between getting paid consistently each month or receiving a quarterly profit distribution, you are going to choose the consistent paycheck. That's why OWNER'S PAY is the first account on your allocation list.

I have the TAX account next. Not PROFIT? One of the biggest problems we see with gym owners is that nasty combination of owing taxes but not having any cash available to cover it. Putting money in your TAX account avoids this problem. Since not paying yourself enough to live and not having any cash for the income tax man are two of the largest cash flow issues, we put a higher priority on these two accounts.

The OWNER'S PAY, TAX, and PROFIT accounts are the cash veggies that benefit you. You allocate to these three accounts first. However, it is possible that you can have too many cash veggies. The health of your gym determines that, and we go into great detail on how you analyze the health of your gym in Chapter 8. At some point in that analysis, you will need to compare what your gym could afford to pay you versus how much you need to take home. Getting you ready for that comparison is what you will learn in the rest of this chapter.

HOW MUCH SHOULD I PAY MYSELF?

You now know that OWNER'S PAY is for you only if you work in the day-to-day of the gym and that PROFIT is for you and all owners. Some people make the mistake of assuming the OWNER'S PAY and PROFIT accounts serve the same purpose. They don't. I emphasize this because your quality of life depends on it.

It is imperative that your lifestyle cost be no higher than the amount of money you take out of your OWNER'S PAY account. You may not rely on your quarterly profit distributions (which come from your PROFIT account) to support your lifestyle. Profit distributions are for celebration and not for day-to-day personal expenses. This doesn't mean you won't achieve a higher quality of life. I have used the last three years of profit distributions to put in a pool, a barbecue area in my backyard, a covered patio, and two fully paid-for brand new cars. My quality of life has definitely increased. But it's important to note that I am not using my profit distributions to put food on the table, cover my mortgage, or keep the lights on at my house.

What if my take-home pay isn't enough for my lifestyle? This could be tough to swallow, but stay the course. You've already committed and you can't turn back now. Your immediate fix is to reduce your personal expenses. The long-term fix is to run the Profit First system which will get your gym financially fit and lead to higher take-home pay.

How do you know if the gym can support your take-home pay? We will explain how to assess this in Chapter 8. At a minimum, you should be able to get market rate for the work you perform. If you're coaching classes, then you should be paid just as a coach would be paid. If you are cleaning the bathrooms and floors, then pay yourself the same amount a cleaner would be paid.

If you aren't paying yourself enough, then chances are the gym's operating expenses are too high. For example, sometimes we hire coaches or additional coaches before our gym can afford them. We hear the advice that in order to grow we need to work *on* our business and not *in* it. So we take the leap and hire people to do the work. Unfortunately, that leap was never meant to be a leap. It's supposed to be more like a hike with multiple steps between the start and the summit. With a healthy gym, you will be able to make this financial hike. You are going to be strategic about how fast you take things off your schedule, freeing up your time in exchange for using cash to pay for that work to be done by someone else.

To find out where you may be spending too much, turn to the Analyze Expenses exercise in Chapter 9. You may find that, in the short run, you need to take some classes back and coach them. You may find other expenses that are unproductive for the business. Your motivation is that every dollar freed up will go toward paying you more money each month.

Is it possible to pay yourself too much? If your gym is running on autopilot, members are having great experiences, and your retention rates are better than industry averages, no. Feel free to overpay yourself. But we have rarely seen that scenario. You may well be overpaying yourself for another reason. And discussing that is never an easy conversation because it basically means the business cannot support your lifestyle.

In that situation, there may not be anything inherently wrong with the gym's finances. It could just be that you have more expensive tastes than you can afford. This could lead to not having enough money to pay your taxes come tax time. It could negatively affect the members' experiences by not having the cash available to meet their needs. Or it could mean you are racking up credit card debt or taking loans and not even realizing you are borrowing money to support your lifestyle.

If you are paying yourself two much, the only two solutions are to increase the gym's Real Revenue so that your current pay is spot on or to cut back on your living expenses. (I'll define Real Revenue shortly.)

No one is asking you to fall on your sword here. You'll never reach your full potential of helping the world if you can't sustain your lifestyle costs on your take-home pay. You deserve to be profitable and to make a great living while helping others. But there are times when lifestyle expectations are unrealistic. So if you are paying yourself too much, all I'm asking is, take a step back and come up with a plan that builds to the lifestyle you expect, like taking an enjoyable hike, instead of a giant leap.

In Chapter 8, you will learn the analysis that reveals if your pay is spot on or if you are paying yourself too little or too much. Before we get to that point, though, it is helpful to know what your current take-home pay needs to cover for your current lifestyle.

A couple of points I want to make before I walk you through how to approach this:

1. What am I *not* asking? I'm not asking you to set up a budget and account for every personal dollar you have spent over the last year so you can tell me what you currently spend each month. Most people who "set up" a budget use that approach. It doesn't work because it feels as if you just

became an accountant. For most people, becoming an accountant is the equivalent of smashing a brick on your face. Repeatedly. Another kerfuffle with this method is, it can reveal how out of control your spending has been. To top it all off, the only thing this accomplishes is telling you what you averaged in spending last year. This is where frustration reaches the boiling point because you wanted to create a budget to stop living paycheck to paycheck and the only thing this approach reveals is your average expenses that resulted *in living paycheck to paycheck.* You wanted to find areas to free up cash, and all you got was an idea of how much you spent.

2. I'm also not asking you to figure out what your perfect day is like. That exercise is designed to help you place a stake in the ground where you want to go. I think that is a worthwhile exercise and a must-do for all gym owners. However, that is not what we are focusing on now. We just want to figure out the smallest amount of money you need from your OWNER'S PAY account.

HOW MUCH ARE YOU SPENDING ON THESE FIVE CATEGORIES?

When figuring out how much you need to support your lifestyle, start by looking at how much money you *should or could* spend in each of the five following categories.

1. Housing Costs: This is your mortgage payment or rent payment. This is also anything else you spend on your house, such as utilities, repairs, home improvements, decorations, cleaning supplies, and any item you consider a household item.

2. Transportation Costs: Car payments or leases and the gas you put in vehicles are the common transportation expenses. However, we have clients who live in New York

City, for example, so they don't own cars. For them, this is likely expenses like the subway, Uber, or taxis.

3. Sustaining Life Costs: We need food to survive, so your groceries are an obvious expense in this category. The typical gym owner also takes a good number of supplements. That expense would also go here. As much as some may want to, you can't really walk around naked all the time, so clothes to cover your nakedness go here. Your personal insurances such as health, life, and disability would also go here. I personally need a massage and chiropractic adjustment at least once per month; those are key for me, so I would put those here. If you don't need something, then it doesn't sustain your life. Also, if I am currently trying to figure out how to lower my lifestyle costs, the massage and adjustment are luxuries that I would need to omit. The same might go for my supplements.

4. Fun Expenses: Anything you do for fun goes in this category. I'm not sure if I have any examples for you because I've been told that, as an accountant, I clearly would never have any idea what humans do for fun.

5. Everything else (miscellaneous): This is your catchall category. Put anything else you spend money on here.

You may be thinking that putting your personal expenses in these five categories seems like the same terrible budget approach I just dismissed. It's different in a couple ways. I'm not asking you to figure out your monthly average expense. I'm asking you to place your expenses into these specific categories because categorizing your expenses will give you clarity as you move to the next step of this process. Further, we aren't just stopping with trying to see what you *have* spent in the past. We will take it a step further and have you ask, "Do I really need this personal expense right now?"

When determining your survival take-home pay, you can eliminate all expenses in the "Fun" and "Everything else" category. Next you need to go through the other expenses and decide if you really need that personal expense to survive. If you are eating out five times a week, maybe cut that back and save some money. Maybe you have health insurance, life insurance, and disability insurance. Look for cheaper options or cut some or all of them for the short run.

Before you add up your expenses, review the numbers one more time. Remember that the point of this exercise is to figure out the smallest amount of money you need each month. I personally like knowing this number because if the stuff hits the fan, I know when to really start stressing. As long as I'm making at least this minimum income number, I can survive.

Now go ahead and add up all those expenses and break the total into a monthly amount. This is your minimum take-home amount.

In Chapter 8, this number will come in handy as we compare what your gym can currently afford to this survival amount. If you already know that your business can't afford your lifestyle, go back and see if you can cut any expenses that aren't absolutely necessary… and I mean ABSOLUTELY necessary.

Over the past twenty years, I've had numerous volunteer experiences with my church in which I sit down with other church members to go over their spending habits. I have seen a lot of justification for expenses that were not ABSOLUTELY necessary to sustain life. So please, if you find yourself in a difficult situation with cash, be honest with yourself.

I promise that if you implement Profit First, any cuts to personal living expenses will be short-term, because you deserve to be profitable and the Profit First method will get you there. What's more, your legacy needs the fuel of profit to survive.

MORE THAN ONE OWNER

When there is only one owner, as difficult as some of those expense-cutting decisions may be, they are much harder when there are two or more gym owners.

How do you determine what each owner should make? Profit First helps us with this difficult decision by taking out any emotions and just relying on the facts. All partners should be valuable to the business. If they aren't, why the crap are they partners in the first place? Since all partners are valuable, all expect to be compensated, and it's easy to think the fair thing to do is to pay all partners equally. No one wants to admit that they aren't pulling their weight or that they are being overpaid for what they are contributing to the business. Profit First fixes all that because it is NOT fair to just blindly pay all partners equally.

OWNER'S PAY only goes toward owners who work in the business. If you have a silent partner, meaning they don't do anything with operations, they should not be paid out of the OWNER'S PAY account.

All the partners need to agree that Profit First is the best thing for them and the most valuable part of their life aside from meeting the love of their life. So once they agree on how amazing Profit First is and have a party to celebrate that they found such a great tool they never want to live without, they then need to agree that the OWNER'S PAY percentages are only paid to owners who work in the business.

Then they need to agree on the pay the partners earn for the different roles and responsibilities they have taken on in the day-to-day operations of the business. If a partner is coaching classes, it makes sense to pay them just as they would pay any other coach. If a partner is acting as the general manager, then they need to agree on fair compensation for the management functions. Each responsibility should be discussed, and an amount which that responsibility earns should be agreed on.

Because the partners should be paid market rates, once profit distributions are high enough it's easier to identify tasks that could be given to other team members.

Remember, the purpose of OWNER'S PAY is different from the purpose of the PROFIT account. The PROFIT account is to reward you for taking the risk of business ownership by providing a return on your investment. OWNER'S PAY is for the partner's day-to-day work in the gym. Profit distributions are to benefit every owner. A silent partner would just get profit distributions, which the partner who is involved in the day-to-day would also get. Profit distributions should be split based on equity ownership. So, if Bob owns 10% and Jimmy owns 90%, and they do a $1,000 profit distribution, Bob gets $100 and Jimmy gets $900.

While the OWNER'S PAY account gives you money every month, profit distributions only happen once each quarter. And when you do a quarterly profit distribution, you will only distribute half of the PROFIT account balance. The remaining half stays in the PROFIT account and should only be used for emergency situations. This becomes a safety net between you and operating paycheck to paycheck.

TOTAL SIDENOTE FOR MATH GEEKS

I once had a microgym owner tell me that the PROFIT account won't work because if you calculate out far enough, the PROFIT account will never become higher than a certain number. So the idea of keeping 50% as a rainy day fund seemed pointless to him because that certain number would never increase to a three-to-six month expense reserve.

So I ran the numbers. Assuming that a gym's monthly income *never* changes and the percentage of income the owner is putting into the PROFIT account *never* changes, then the highest balance that would eventually be in the PROFIT account would be eight times the PROFIT account percentage multiplied by the never-changing monthly income. Boy, that's a mouthful. Let's say the gym will always and forever have $10,000 in monthly income. Let's say the profit percentage is 3%. Eight times the profit percentage of 3% is 24%. And 24% of 10,000 is $2,400. So the PROFIT account in this case would never be higher than $2,400.

La-de-da. The system still works. And if the above facts were true, having $2,400 set aside for an emergency is better than having nothing set aside. And there is also the $4,800 of profit distributions sent to the owners each year.

FINANCIAL WORKOUT

Growing up, the only vegetable I was really exposed to was corn. (Yeah. I know.) To get us to eat broccoli, my mom would blend the broccoli and put in other things. I am only a little bit better today as an adult. Veggies just don't taste that good to me. But I do have one favorite veggie. The cash veggie! It's so delicious and is an important component of being financially fit. This financial workout is critical to your financially fit plan as well. Regularly consuming your cash veggies will also reduce the inflammation we can feel sometimes after working really hard and not feeling as though we have anything to show for it.

Figure out your survival take-home pay. It will make the Chapter 8 analysis so much easier. If your current take-home pay is more than the minimum amount you've figured out, and your gym is comfortably paying it, then feel free to stick with that number. If you have more than one owner working in the gym, define your roles and responsibilities and determine the pay rate for each. This reduces any possible friction that may exist between you and your partner(s) that blindly equal pay causes.

CHAPTER 6

REMOVE TEMPTATION

T EMPTATION HAS BEEN WITH US FROM THE BEGINNING OF THE earth when Adam and Eve partook of the Tree of Knowledge of Good and Evil. God forbade them to eat the fruit, and Satan tempted them to eat the fruit. Since that first temptation, there have been more than six quadrillion temptations as of record. (Not a real statistic, by the way.)

Temptation as defined in the dictionary is a desire to do something, especially something wrong or unwise. And if you think about the way we use the word, you don't usually hear people say things like, "hey, don't tempt me into doing a good deed," or, "I was almost tempted to say something nice," or, "oh yeah, if you tempt me I'll eat the whole plate of broccoli."

For me it's usually, "Is that a peanut butter and jelly sandwich? Boy that makes me want a Reese's." It doesn't matter which holiday is coming up, they all end with me eating the special Reese's of the season. Reese's bunnies, Reese's eggs, Reese's half-pound cups, Reese's shaped like a giant heart. Basically, everything for me triggers a desire to Reese's. Why? Probably because I might be a sugar addict.

You probably already know that it's proven that people can become addicted to sugar. One research study[1] looked at the addictive nature of sugar by depriving rats of food for twelve hours and then, for the next twelve, giving them access to sugar water. They found that, rather quickly, the rats started showing signs of addiction. They concluded

---

[1] Magalie Lenoir, Fuschia Serre, Lauriane Cantin, Serge Ahmed; "Intense Sweetness Surpasses Cocaine Reward," Aug 1, 2007, https://www.ncbi.nlm.nih.gov, accessed November 24, 2019

that not only can you have a sugar addiction, but also that sugar surpasses cocaine in addictive power.

Many, many, many people have relied on that research and have even written books about the dangers of sugar addiction. In 2016, the University of Cambridge decided to research[2] the validity of the previous sugar addiction study. They didn't do their own study. They just looked at the data from the rat study, picked apart the approach the researchers used, and decided that sugar is not an addictive substance. Apparently, I'm crazy because so many everyday things trigger a desire to stuff my face with half-pound Reese's peanut butter cups. Why do I bring this up? Well, we were talking about temptation, and sugar is a real temptation for me, and screw you, University of Cambridge.

The truth is, whether or not research confirms sugar addiction is real, it's real for me. You see this with your clients and their own food addictions and temptations every day. You also see this with yourself—and I'm not talking about food. As I thought about conversations I've had with hundreds of microgym owners, I came up with this list of common temptations gym owners fall for. (Don't worry. I'll keep this PG-13.)

1. **Blind Leading the Blind (Copycatting Others)**
   How did you figure out what to charge for membership fees and training? When I ask this question of clients, I usually get some version of, "Well, I looked at what the guy down the road is doing and matched what he is charging." Well, how did he figure it out? He did the same thing. This process of just doing what someone else is doing has been repeated thousands of times. I think you understand that not all gym owners actually know what they are doing. Yet, it's easy to be tempted to fall in line with what other people do. Your

---

[2] Max Shinn, "Is Sugar Addictive? Probably Not, Say Cambridge Neuroscientists," *University of Cambridge,* July 21, 2016, https://www.psychiatry.cam.ac.uk/blog/2016/07/21/sugar-addictive-probably-not-say-cambridge-neuroscientists, accessed November 24, 2019

prices, the number of locations you choose to have, how big or small each location should be, marketing messages and where you choose to advertise—basically every aspect of creating and running your gym could be based on how other microgym owners set up their businesses. I know it's tempting to follow the example of others, especially if we perceive them as more successful than us, but don't do this blindly or automatically.

2. **Novelty Equipment**

   Atlas stones. Gigantic tires. Sleds. Sandbags. Peg boards. I've been to quite a few gyms and these items are always just sitting there, covered in dust and cobwebs. Okay, maybe just dust, but a lot of dust. Most of our members just want to look better naked, and basic gym equipment is all they need to achieve that goal. Deep down, the gym owners know this, since they haven't found ways to include the shiny objects in the workouts. The hard truth is, we are tempted to buy new equipment thinking it alone will bring in more revenue. It won't.

3. **Ignore Accounting**

   Most people think of accounting as something that has to get done so they can file their tax returns, which is why they view accounting as an annual event. They think of it as an *event* because they give up a few weekends in a row, or a few business days, to "get ready" for their meeting with their CPA, about the same amount of time they would spend attending a training or conference. Are you worried about your money? Are you interested in what your money is doing? Where your money is going? How you are getting money? Guess what, that's what accounting tells you. The temptation here is that you likely don't enjoy accounting so you will choose to do *anything* else if it means you don't have to go cross-eyed staring at your accounting. Taking the time throughout the year (smaller meals more frequently) will make this feel less of a burden and more of a blessing.

4. **Handshake Deals**

The last thing we want to do is offend a friend. The second-to-last thing we want to do is offend someone who could be a friend someday. We want to avoid conflict whenever possible. As a gym owner, you want team members you can rely on. Well, who better than a trusted friend? But we don't want conflict with the friend, and discussing money may lead to conflict. We talk around what their services are worth and what you think your services are worth. The last thing we would want to do is put it clearly in writing because that could lead to a disagreement. Enter the handshake deal. This keeps both you and the friend (or, fingers crossed, future friend) from getting on the same page. It's guaranteed they understand the nature of the relationship differently than you do. Always have a contract. With your friends and future friends (coaches, team members, business partners, gym members). Always. Contracts are great because you set them up when both sides are happy. Because if one side becomes angry (I know, it would never happen to you), that contract gives you the best chance of a fair outcome.

Another nature of a handshake deal is the service swap. This can be problematic. It works like this. If you clean the gym, I'll give you your membership for free. Great. Let's shake on it. When swapping services, I have found that *both* parties feel as if they are getting screwed. The best solution to this is just *don't do it*. You clean the gym, and I'll pay you. You come to classes, and you'll pay me for those services. The next best solution is to have a contract. Here is the checklist for cleaning the gym. Here are our expectations on time commitment. If you do not complete all the tasks or meet your time commitment, we will credit the work done toward your membership, but it will not be a straight swap. It's because you are my friend and I want to stay friends that we need a contract. Handshake deals help us avoid uncomfortable situations up front. That's why we are tempted by them. An uncomfortable conversation up front can save you the possibility of financial loss and friendship loss in the long run.

5. **Marketing**

   Some gym owners fall into the trap of believing the right marketing event will magically transform their gym into the type of business they have fantasized about since they first got the idea to open their doors. I haven't seen one single marketing event accomplish this. Don't be tempted to overspend on your marketing budget. Be smart about how you spend your marketing dollars and always, always, always track the results. If you can't track the result of a marketing campaign, don't do it. If you don't have a marketing budget, then you definitely don't want to fall for the salesman offering a shiny piece of crap in a box... but at least it has a guarantee, right, Tommy Boy? With Profit First, we focus a lot on controlling the cash outflow to get to profitability. However, we understand that increasing revenue helps also. The abundance of opportunities to grow our revenue number is what makes the single marketing event so tempting. As we try to fill our drinking glass (increase sales), the glass will never get to full when we have holes everywhere. Two holes to plug before ever spending money on marketing: First, if you don't have a good onboarding system to turn leads into members, then it doesn't matter what you spend on marketing, and, second, if you don't have good retention of current members, then any marketing spend is just flushing your cash down the toilet. Growth comes much more from retention than it does new leads.

The Association of Fitness Studios found the average retention rate for a microgym (they call it a fitness studio) is 75.9%[3] and Madlab founder Craig "Patty" Patterson did his own study with ZenPlanner where he found the yearly retention rate for microgyms only offering group classes to be just 25%.[4] That is obviously way worse than 75.9%. Using the higher retention rate means, if you start the year with one hundred members and do nothing else during the year, you would have seventy-five members left at the end of the year. That's twenty-five former members not paying you anymore. Lost members mean lost revenue, which means lost profitability. If your average monthly revenue is $150, that's $3,750 of monthly revenue gone or $45,000 per year. Now you have to spend time and resources from a smaller pool to replace those twenty-five lost members. Consider now if you were able to add twenty-five new members and your retention rate is 85%[5] like the Madlab School of Fitness. That means with one hundred members you only lose fifteen. Add twenty-five new members and you are at one hundred and ten. In this example, the only difference is retention. Retain and grow.

PROFIT FIRST TEMPTATIONS

As you start living the Profit First method, two of your bank account balances will be higher than your other accounts: the **PROFIT** account and the **TAX** account. Why is that? The **TAX** account accumulates because you deposit money into it each month, but, since you pay your taxes annually or quarterly you only have one or four withdrawals a year. The purpose of the **TAX** account is to cover the tax burden your business profits generate, not to bail you out of poorly chosen

[3] Chuck Leve, "Why Your Retention Rate is the Key to Understanding Fitness Business Success," Association of Fitness Studios, https://member.afsfitness.com, accessed November 24, 2019

[4] MadLab Group, "Zen Planner study on Retention and ACV Episode 47," https://www.crowdcast.io/e/the-gymmin-made-easy-12, accessed November 24, 2019

[5] Craig Patterson, "Show us the data!" June 26, 2019, https://madlabgroup.com/show-us-data, *Madlab Group*, accessed November 24, 2019

expenses. If you aren't careful, you may be tempted to use the TAX account to cover operating expenses when you are short on cash.

You already know that the purpose of the PROFIT account is to give you a return on investment for taking the risk of business ownership. Because it only has one distribution each quarter, it, too, will accumulate money quickly. If you are in a cash crunch, you may want to raid the PROFIT account. It's important to remember that that money is your personal reward for ownership and should never be used to cover operating expenses.

In *Profit First*, Mike recommends opening two accounts in a totally separate bank so that you are less likely to pull money from them: one for your income taxes and the other for your profit. The objective is to make it as inconvenient as possible to access the money. No debit cards. No checks. No online access. If your account has a convenience feature, turn it off. Ideally, you want to have to drive to the bank in order to pull cash out.

If Mike and I are asking you to set up these accounts at a different bank, you may be wondering why you need a TAX and PROFIT account at your main bank if the money is only going to be in there for a few hours or a day. The main reason is because of the timing of such transfers. It's possible that when you make the transfer or write an actual check to your "no temptation" bank, that the money could still show as available at your main bank for a few days. Without separate accounts, that cash would be sitting in your OPEX account showing it's available to spend. However, the money is not available; it's already been spoken for.

Really though, setting up "no temptation" accounts protects you from yourself. If you end up in a situation where you have more bills to pay than what you have available in your OPEX account, you cannot steal from yourself and take money from your TAX account or PROFIT account. This doesn't solve the problem, and you may miss the lesson the business is trying to teach you, which may be that you have some bills that you shouldn't. Maybe you need to cut back so you can afford just the necessary things right now instead of the "nice to have" things.

NO-TEMPTATION ACCOUNTS
RECOMMENDED, NOT REQUIRED

You are likely not going to set up separate accounts, though. Our firm works with more microgyms than any other tax, accounting, bookkeeping, or Profit First firm in the country, and we noticed that most of our boutique and microgym clients did not have a separate bank account set up.

In addition, we polled a large group of more than four hundred microgym owners who have watched our Profit First training videos and asked them if they are using the "no-temptation" accounts at a separate bank. Only two of them were using the accounts. Two. Just two. One of the two said he did it because that is what the book recommends, but he doesn't think it actually helps him.

Here are the reasons given us for not setting up the "no temptation" accounts:

- It's a hassle setting up the accounts.
- It's too hard to find a bank with the limited conveniences required for these two accounts.
- Seeing the large balances isn't a temptation, and the idea of dipping into that cash just doesn't happen.
- It is encouraging to see the two accounts grow. A business owner should see that progress.
- I just hide the balances on my main screen online and that does the same thing for me.
- I have discipline, so I can handle the temptation.
- Too many extra bank fees.
- I don't want to manage more accounts at a different bank. Keeping things simple is better.

I don't want to simply throw aside this list of reasons, and I'm purposely using the word *reasons* here and not the word *excuses*. Most gym owners are using the above reasons to not open accounts at a separate bank, despite the fact that they work the other parts of the Profit First system.

The reason setting up "no temptation" accounts is a core principle is because most business owners live paycheck to paycheck. Before finding us, most gym owners don't have enough cash to run their business, let alone set aside for profit, so there is no temptation to mismanage their cash flow because there isn't any cash to manage. This system can make any business profitable, and an increase in cash balances is a natural consequence. Enter the possibility to be tempted. The system cannot work if the gym owner is going to take money that has been set aside for tax payments or profit distributions and use them to cover operating expenses.

I can totally get behind the idea of not having a separate bank for these accounts. I think seeing these two accounts grow month after month is encouraging. It would motivate me or at least serve as a reminder that what we are doing is still working. Even though I wouldn't use the money in that account for anything other than its purpose of tax or profit, seeing the balance grow does provide a level of confidence that I have found translates into better business decisions.

Plus, if you've made a commitment to the Profit First way, you are going to follow through on that commitment. It is very possible that you won't see a high balance in your tax or profit account as a temptation. You have funds in the other accounts as well, which you aren't taking money from except for the designated purpose. So why should these two accounts be any different?

Although removing temptation is a core principle of *Profit First*, it is not a requirement of *Profit First for Microgyms* that you have these two accounts at a separate bank. Still, consider these three reasons setting up these accounts.

Obviously, if you are unsure or already know if these accounts will tempt you, then you need separate accounts at a separate institution.

If you don't think it's a big deal to manage two more accounts at a different bank, and you find one of the many options of free accounts, then I say do this step.

If you like the idea of earning a little bit better interest rate on the cash that sits in these accounts, there are some great money market or other liquid types of accounts that can get you a better return than what you get in the account at your main bank.

FINANCIAL WORKOUT

Temptations are all around us. Consider the common temptations I shared in this chapter and see if you may be allowing any of them to affect your profitability: copycatting others, buying novelty equipment, ignoring the importance of accounting, handshake deals, and spending money on marketing when conversion or retention rates are bad.

Determine which camp you sit in. Are you going to be tempted or not? Do you fit into one of the three reasons to have a separate account? How committed are you to not steal from yourself? (Because that is what you do when you use cash in these two accounts for anything other than taxes or profit distributions.)

Once you know your answer, go get these accounts set up. Or don't.

CHAPTER 7

EAT SMALLER MEALS
MORE FREQUENTLY

ATING SMALLER MEALS MORE FREQUENTLY ALLOWS YOU TO consume fewer calories per meal than you would if you ate two or three big meals each day. It also allows your body to avoid feeling hungry. The person who feels hungry has a much greater chance of making a poor eating decision than the person who doesn't. (I will neither confirm nor deny how much personal experience I have with that.)

Eating smaller meals throughout the day requires a rhythm. We aren't talking about eating breakfast, skipping lunch, and then having dinner, dessert, seconds of dinner, and seconds of dessert. That's really two big meals. I'm talking about having nearly the same amount of time between meals throughout the day. This way the hunger levels stay in check. Breakfast, mid-morning snack, lunch, mid-afternoon snack, dinner, and evening snack. By having roughly three hours between each meal, you create a pattern.

We need a similar healthy rhythm for managing our cash. What does rhythm mean? The definition I like from www.lexico.com is a strong, regular, repeated pattern of movement or sound. When thinking about this we often think about dancing or music, or of double unders, or the feel of the hollow body and head through the window for linking pull-ups, toes to bar, and muscle ups. However, rhythm can be just as applicable in the context of our habits.

In his book, *The Power of Habit*, Charles Duhigg explains that each habit starts with a cue that triggers a routine that leads to a reward. That reward causes your brain to pay more attention to the cue, which makes your triggers more appealing and stronger as time goes on. There is a rhythm to that process. Your cues are strong, and, when you receive whatever cue it is, you take action and repeat that behavior every time you are cued to do so.

Again, the definition of rhythm is a strong, regular, repeated pattern of movement. An action is a movement. So we are talking about movements *or actions* that have those three characteristics.

A rhythm is a strong action, not a weak action. This means there has to be a level of commitment. If you've ever done a workout that involves box jumps, a simple fact is easy to overlook: You know that if you are *not* committed every time, you could end up with really bloody shins.

A rhythm is a regular action, not a sporadic action. If I want to improve on a muscle-up, sporadically working on it a couple times a year is not going to help me. If you want to learn about your cash flow in your gym, looking at it once per year is not going to help. The action of looking at it needs to be regular.

A rhythm is a repeated action, not a "re-invent the wheel every time" action. When managing your cash flow, you want to go through the same steps each time you sit down to look at it. Dedicating a regular time to do it is not enough. You have to make sure you are looking at the cash the same way each time.

THE CASH FLOW RHYTHM

As a microgym owner you already have evidence of how a rhythm can be beneficial: exercise and meal planning. Your members who see the greatest gain are more than likely the ones who have a rhythm to their workout behavior: strong, regular, repeated. You probably know what days of the week to expect them and even which class they are going to attend. You've probably seen other members who maybe were consistent for a time and then once, they fell off the habit, it took them forever to get back into a routine—or maybe they never did. The contrast between those two situations highlights how a rhythm can make all the difference.

A rhythm in your dieting also helps. I know that the most success I had in losing weight was when I had planned out meals *and* I actually planned out when I was going to make those meals. I got into a rhythm, and the plan helped me stay in rhythm. When I don't plan out my meals, my diet consists of Reese's, fast food, and Oreos. When I do plan my meals, I know that Sunday and Wednesday are good evenings for me to get my meals together. It's important for me to keep about the same amount of time between meal prep days.

How does this relate to managing your cash flow? You need a rhythm to your accounting and to your Profit First system. Instead of the sporadic and occasional approach most owners take to their accounting, you, my friend, are going to have a system. No one wants to look like *Seinfeld*'s beloved Elaine Benes when she dances. That is literally the opposite of rhythm.

There are four main tasks you want to accomplish on each Rhythm Day.

1. Calculate Real Revenue.
2. Move money from your INCOME account to the other smaller plate bank accounts.
3. Determine what bills to pay.
4. Actually pay the bills.

The rhythm we recommend with Profit First is called the 10/25 Rhythm, which refers to focusing on bookkeeping on the 10th and the 25th of each month. This puts roughly fifteen days between each sit-down between you and your cash. We have clients who use other days, such as the 5th and 20th because that coincides with their payroll days, but the general idea is that you want fifteen days between each Rhythm Day.

In very rare situations, it may make sense to increase the frequency to once per week. We had a client get in trouble with sales tax. In order for him to be compliant with his payment plan with the state, the easiest way was to have his Rhythm Day once each week when he also would make a weekly payment on his sales tax obligation.

Focusing on cash flow once per week is the most someone should be doing. It should never be more than once per week. One of the microgym owners we work with was getting really frustrated with the Profit First system. No matter what we did or tried, he still felt as though it was way too much work, which is really the opposite of what typically happens. Once properly implemented, Profit First reduces the amount of time spent on accounting and cash flow, and certainly reduces the "brain damage" that pre-Profit First life caused. So, this client's feelings didn't make sense to us. When we really dug into what he was doing, we quickly saw that he was doing Rhythm Days every workday, about twenty times per month. Good grief! Of course that seems like too much work, because *it is* too much work. After he saw the error of his ways, he fell in love with the system and started seeing the benefits of freeing up time while being more organized.

WHAT IS REAL REVENUE?

Real Revenue is a Profit First term that I want to become part of your DNA. You have probably heard about Gross Revenue or Total Revenue or maybe just simply Revenue. Or you could call it Gross Sales, Total Sales, or Sales. Those accounting terms refer to the exact same number (at least they should be referring to the same number). That is not what we are talking about. Real Revenue is not Total Revenue or Gross Revenue, and it certainly isn't fake revenue. (We've all met those people who can't help but blow smoke with "how good they are doing" when in reality they are doing terribly.)

Real Revenue is your Total Revenue minus your materials and subcontractors expense. That is how Mike defined it in the original *Profit First* book. His intention in creating this metric was so that companies across industries could more accurately compare themselves. More importantly, Real Revenue allowed any company in any industry the ability to use the Profit First table that provides the basis of what percentages you should be transferring to your smaller plate bank accounts.

Imagine you are talking to an owner of a construction company, and he tells you that he has a $2 million business. Color me impressed! You can clearly see that this owner is living as though he has a $2 million business. What he is not telling you is that he is in debt up to his eyeballs, he lives paycheck to paycheck, he's constantly pushing his credit card limits, and the bank has already started the process of repossessing his tricked-out truck. How does this happen?

Real Revenue explains it for us. This guy's business has Total Revenue of $2 million. He built four houses to earn that income, though not with his own bare hands. He hired project managers, subcontractors, foundation guys, framers, electricians, plumbers. Sometimes he purchased the lumber and materials and sometimes his contractors purchased the materials and passed the cost on to him. The bottom line is he had $1.8 million in costs just to earn the $2 million in Total Revenue. His Real Revenue is only $200,000. He's acting like a $2 million-dollar business when he is really only a $200,000 business.

Now that we have a reference point of Real Revenue, we could compare the $200,000 construction company to a $200,000 gym. Both owners would be able to use the Profit First table to determine how much to allocate to each small plate bank account. Both would have similar take-home pay, profit distributions, and tax allocations.

Here is the glorious thing about this very book you hold in your hands: I am going to explain to you how this concept specifically applies to your microgym. The challenge Mike had in having many businesses across many industries is not my challenge. I am talking to you, a boutique and microgym owner.

Real Revenue for a microgym is Total Revenue minus the cost of apparel, supplements, and beverages you sell. That's it. We are not going to include the cost of your coaches to get to Real Revenue. Why? Because it got too complicated. Some coaches are employees. Some coaches are independent contractors. Some are paid a salary, some are paid an hourly rate, some are paid per class, and some are paid a percentage of the income they generate. An independent contractor who gets paid per class could go under Real Revenue, but an employee who gets a salary wouldn't. However, if you paid an employee per class, then you would put that in Real Revenue. What if the coach does some personal training and they are paid a percentage of that income, but they also get a salary to coach group classes? We discovered that the sky was the limit on the different and creative structures gym owners came up with paying their coaches. Each situation needed analysis and explanation from our team which put us into "accountant speak" and no one wants to hear that. We want "human speak."

Let's say you pay coach Kelly $20 per group class and 50 percent for personal training sessions. She teaches one group class and has three personal training sessions, which bring in $180. For sake of this example, let's say the group class has five members, and they were all drop-ins who paid $15 each. The gym's Total Revenue would be $255 ($75 from the group class + $180 for the personal training sessions) on Kelly's efforts. You pay Kelly $110: $90 (which is her 50 percent of the $180) + $20 for the group class. The Real Revenue on these services would be $145 ($255 – $110). If coach Kelly doesn't provide any service, the gym doesn't make any revenue *and* coach Kelly wouldn't make any money either. However, because she provides the service, the gym makes money and owes money to Kelly for her services.

Contrast that with this scenario: Now coach Kelly makes $22 per hour. She is at the gym from five a.m. to ten a.m., for five hours. During those five hours, she coaches one group class and teaches three personal training sessions. As was the case in the first example, the gym makes $255 in revenue for those five hours and Kelly's pay is $110 (five hours at $22 per hour). The gym's Real Revenue in this situation would be $255 and not $145. The reason is that the cost of providing the services is not directly tied to the earning of the income. If coach Kelly weren't there, someone else would have been, and if the members weren't there for the services, Coach Kelly still makes $110 for her hourly pay.

You see, too complicated. Bleh! To simplify this, we just took it out of the Real Revenue calculation and gave team member cost its own spot on the Profit First for Microgyms table.

Real Revenue is important because it shows us how our gym should act. A startup gym needs to act differently from a gym in growth mode, which needs to act differently from an established gym. (In his book, *Founder, Farmer, Tinker, Thief,* Chris Cooper offers a lot of

Before:	After:
PROFIT ASSESSMENT	**CASH FLOW ANALYSIS**
Top Line Revenue	Top Line Revenue
Materials & Subcontractors	Cost of Items You Sell
Real Revenue	Real Revenue
Profit	Team Members
Owner's Pay	Profit
Tax	Owner's Pay
Operating	Tax
	Equipment
	Operating Expenses

business advice based on the specific growth stages of a gym. Read his book too.)

A gym that only has $60,000 in Real Revenue needs to act differently from a gym that has $250,000 in Real Revenue. Now, I'm not talking about the fundamental things that all successful microgyms have in common, such as standard operating procedures or having one-on-one meetings with prospects to discover how your gym can best serve them. A great many business coaches and mentors for microgyms can go over those fundamental things you need to do. That's their expertise. My expertise is with all things cash flow, which is why you are reading this book. You want more of it and, believe me, you have a right to it based on all the good you do for your members. Profit First makes sure you can keep doing that good.

From a cash flow standpoint, a $60,000 gym has to behave differently from a $250,000 gym. The table in Chapter 8 breaks out the common percentages that should be allocated to each smaller plate bank account based on the dollar amount of Real Revenue. These are your Current Allocation Percentages (CAPs). In Chapter 8 we will go over the specifics of how to use the allocation table. The main point I wanted to make with this introduction to Real Revenue is that Gross Revenue can be deceiving whereas Real Revenue provides a more accurate picture of the financial size of your gym.

With Real Revenue calculated, you will now move the correct amounts of money from your INCOME account into your OWNER'S PAY, PROFIT, and TAX accounts, in that order. That way we are eating our veggies first. Then, transfer funds into your TEAM MEMBER account, EQUIPMENT account and then into your OPEX account. Again, how much you should transfer into each of those accounts will be determined by your CAPs.

DETERMINE WHICH BILLS YOU WILL PAY

The process of transferring money using your CAPs is half of what Rhythm Days are about. Now that you have transferred to your different accounts, you can see how much cash you have available to pay bills. Let me tell you how glorious this is! Here I go: This is glorious. Why is it glorious? Let's think about how bills are usually handled. When a bill comes in, if the owner thinks they have enough cash in their account, they usually pay it. Sometimes the owner even logs into their bank account to check the balance. If the balance is high enough, the bill gets paid. If the balance is always high enough, the gym owner will pay bills all through the month whenever a bill shows up in the mail. If the balance is low, the bill gets placed somewhere. I say somewhere, because it's uncommon for a gym owner to have an organized filing system for their bills. This unpaid bill becomes like a tiny pebble that gets in your shoe when you are hiking. It starts to feel a lot bigger than it is. It takes up space in your subconscious as it silently annoys the crap out of you. It's something else on your to-do list now and it's also going to take money out of your pocket. This is the stuff gray hairs are made of. Maybe after a reminder from the vendor or when the owner randomly comes across the bill again, when the bank balance is checked, and there is enough money., it finally gets paid. Bottom line is that this unpaid bill took up way too much brain space and energy.

Here is the new way of paying your bills, Profit First style. It is a simpler method, yet so elegant. When you receive a bill, set it aside in a specific location. The location is so specific that you will use the same location every time for all bills. For me, it's a corner of my desk that is out of my line of sight. I give that bill no other thought. I simply place it in its home and do the same with every new bill coming in. What if the bill was emailed to you? Not a problem. Create a folder in your email and call it "Bills to Pay." Store your e-bills here.

Then, on your Rhythm Day, pull out your stack of bills and e-bills and organize them from most past due to the farthest-off due date. Any bill that isn't due until after the next allocation day automatically goes back into the stack. So if today is the 10th, my next allocation day is the 25th. Any bill that is due on the 25th or after is going back on the stack. I'm not wasting any more time thinking about it.

With the remaining stack, add up the dollar amount needed to pay all of them. Since you've already allocated your income into the smaller plate accounts, you can see how much is in your OPEX account balance. If the balance is high enough to cover all the bills, then go ahead and pay them. (I like to have a cushion in my OPEX account that I don't want to drop below.)

PAY YOUR BILLS

As unlikely as it may seem, it is possible that the cash needed to pay current bills might be more than what is available in your OPEX account. This is when you need to remind yourself of your commitment to be profitable. The temptation to dip into any of the other accounts to cover the remaining bills will be real. Gym owners seem to start with their OWNER'S PAY account. Don't do that. Things will get better, and, even if this is the current situation, it too shall pass. (One of my dad's favorite lines.) You are just going to have some bills that are paid late and you may even be making calls to your vendors to let them know they aren't going to be paid on time. I am not suggesting that you never pay these bills. You made a commitment and you'll pay them. It just isn't happening on time.

Mike explained it this way, "If you take money from your PROFIT account and put it back into the business, you are basically saying that you are unwilling to find a way to run your business with the operating expenses you allocated for it. The bottom line is this: don't cut your salary to make the numbers work. Your martyr syndrome is not doing anyone any favors; making yourself the sacrificial lamb does not promote efficiency; it hinders it."

The truth is, if you were speaking to Mike in a moment of possible temptation, he would probably beg you to not steal from *any* of the accounts. He would urge you to dig deep and get creative instead of taking the easy way out.

When you owe more in bills than you have available in your OPEX account, you need to determine which bills are the most important to pay right now. Decide which bills help you keep the doors open. Remember that your team member costs were already taken care of because you allocated money into that separate bank account, because that is an important cash outflow for your gym. .

This is super important because it will reveal the expenses that aren't actually needed to keep your doors open. Your business is screaming at you that you have too many expenses and it can't afford all of them. If, during this process, you find yourself putting off paying a specific bill more often than other bills, chances are you should cancel that expense.

WHAT'S IN IT FOR ME?

One benefit from establishing this rhythm is that you will identify trends in your business. You'll start to know when you expect your income to come in and which time of the month you'll have more bills to pay. You'll even start to see yearly cycles. For example, after doing this cash flow system in my own business, I know in which months I expect to see lower revenue and in which months to expect higher revenue. I know when I have large expenses coming so I am better at planning for those now. You will also benefit because you will find that you think less about what bills you have due throughout the month.

Maybe you worry about your cash flow on a regular basis. You may feel it as a constant nagging in the very back of your mind, just annoyingly scratching at you, day in and day out. With Rhythm Days, that nagging thought should go away. You now know and your subconscious now knows that you have a dedicated day to think about that. I don't think about bills at all anymore except on the 10th and 25th when I'm sitting down to pay them. This change allows me to stay focused on other work the rest of the month. My mind is crisper. You are going to notice the same benefits and it is GLORIOUS TO BEHOLD!

THREE RULES OF ORGANIZATION

At my microgym and others I've visited, when the workout is over, everyone cleans up their equipment. In our gym, each piece of equipment has its own home, and all our members know where those places are. We ask them to do this so future classes can also find the equipment. This is one of the rules of organization.

At a Profit First training, Andrew Mellon, who claims to be the most organized man in the world, laid out the three rules of organization.

1. Like with Like (items are stored with the same types of items).
2. Something in, Something out (helps avoid hoarding).
3. Everything has one home.

When your members clean up after a workout, it's easy for them because they know where everything goes. Medicine balls are placed with the other medicine balls. Yoga mats are stored with the other yoga mats. You put 45-pound weight plates with the other 45-pound weight plates. Like with Like.

What about your money? Often we use overgeneralizations when we think about money. It's our money, and we think about it just like that: one category we refer to as "our money." By now, you know that isn't completely accurate. Deposits made to your business account *(please be to your business account and not your personal account)* aren't really considered your money. You made a commitment to coaches, so some of the deposits belong to them. You have a contract with the landlord, so some of the deposits belong to them. My least favorite relative, Uncle Sam, (or, as I like to call him, Satan) worked out a deal where he gets to take some of that money, so some of the deposits are ~~stolen~~ taken by him. We could take that example to a very detailed and thorough place, but we will leave it at that. You get the point.

Your money isn't one category of things, but lots of categories of things. Just as we don't want 10-pound plates in our 45-pound plate stack or yoga mats with the kettle bells, we don't want our rent money with our take-home pay. You know the solution because you already learned it. The smaller plates. The Essential Seven Accounts, which you learned about in Chapter 4.

1. Your Profit should have a separate home. What's the point of being in business if your business isn't rewarding you with some profit?
2. Your pay for working in the business needs a special place. You will always be your most important employee, and the most important employee *must* get paid.
3. Your tax obligation should be set aside in a separate account. I hate it and I spend most of my days helping people minimize it, but it is an absolute in life. You pay taxes. So it's better to just set it aside as you go about the year than to hope you won't have to pay anything.
4. Your income gets deposited into a separate account with all the other income because those dollars need to be named and defined by transferring them to the other smaller plates.
5. Your team members represent one of your highest expenses; we have a separate home for our commitment to them just so we'll know that we have it when we need it.
6. Your members are hard on your equipment. Those items are not going to last forever. We like the idea of setting aside money each month into a separate bank account that is used for repairs and new purchases of equipment.

7. Your business operating expense is the last thing that should have its own account. Most of your transactions will probably run through it.

Placing your money into different homes, makes things simpler. I know it seems counterintuitive when you first look at that list. How can having more bank accounts make things simpler? For starters, most of these new accounts will have a small number of transactions. Also, imagine if everything in your gym didn't have a home. One giant pile of barbells, weight plates, jump ropes, rowers, assault bikes, wall balls, mats, chalk, sandbags. It would be terrible! Well, that is what we are doing when we only have one bank account.

ORGANIZING YOUR TIME

The rules of organization not only apply to physical things, but also to the non-physical. For example, I like to organize my time to stress. Yes, you read that right. I know I'm going to stress, so I'd rather take control of when that is going to happen. I'm not saying I can predict that on Tuesday I'm going to be stressed at 3:02 p.m. But I do know what things make me stressed. Payroll day stresses me out. So I purposely don't have payroll on my Rhythm Days.

This idea of organizing my stress is more than just scheduling stressful activities. It's also about organizing to avoid things. I have scheduling rules to never have two appointments in a row. The thing that probably stresses me out the most is going an entire day being busy and accomplishing nothing. You've been there, you felt really busy but can't remember a single thing you did. That happens to me when I don't have a good plan, so I set aside time at the end of the day to plan for tomorrow.

What might you be stressing about? If you are like most boutique and microgym owners, you probably stress about paying bills, and that stress isn't necessarily related to, "Do I have enough money for my bills?" The stress can also come in the form of constantly thinking about them, even if there is enough money to pay them.

Your Profit First system can take away this stress when you simply do your Rhythm Days. When you set aside a regular time to pay bills and review cash flow, you can decrease your stress and worry about having enough money for bills and constantly thinking about them.

You see this principle in the lives of your members. They just have to show up for the workout. No stress is required. Most of our members, like myself, have no desire to ever be a professional exerciser. We exercise to be healthy. And most of our members, like myself, would never do any workouts at home because we stress about what workout we should be doing. Which muscle group should I work out? Have I overworked something? Should I just lift weights? Should I just train to run a marathon? Your gym takes all this stress away by telling them exactly what to do during the workout. All they have to do is show up.

Having a set time to pay bills and review cash flow accomplishes the same thing. I don't think about my bills unless it is that scheduled time. I've been using a scheduled time for almost three years now and I can tell you it is GLORIOUS! (Have I said that yet?) My bills get paid. My team members get paid. I identify expenses that were useless and I only think about it twice per month. The rest of the time I can think about whatever I want and I can worry about whatever I want. I know whatever I *do* choose to stress out about, it *ain't* about money.

FREQUENCY DOESN'T ALWAYS INDICATE IMPORTANCE

One exercise movement we don't do too often at our gym is the sumo deadlift high pull. I love the movement of the sumo deadlift high pull. It feels good. It makes me concentrate on a lot of different things that, in turn, make my other movements better. Flex your quads and butt cheeks. Shrug. Keep your core tight. Don't overextend your back when you bring your elbows high and keep your core tight as you lower. I love all that. Plus, having injured my lower back previously, I really appreciate that the sumo stance alleviates some of the lower back movement compared to a normal stance. However, despite all of its benefits, we only do it a few times a year. This got me thinking about what things you might find yourself doing only once or twice a year. Just because we only do it once or twice a year doesn't make that activity or action any less important than something you do every day. The activity that comes to mind is repairing and buying equipment. It's just not something that happens often. Because it doesn't happen very often, it seems as though it always catches us off guard. Maybe the rower breaks. Or our climbing ropes look more like decorative streamers. Or our 10-pound plates have trashed hubs. The list goes on and on. Members are not gentle on our equipment, to say the least. Or maybe your membership is growing, and your class size is so big that you don't have enough rowers or bikes for everyone or pull up bars, or rings, and so on. We will eventually have to buy more equipment. Or repair our equipment. So plan for it.

This is why you have an EQUIPMENT account as part of your Essential Seven Accounts. Its sole purpose is having money set aside for equipment costs. Each time you sit down for a Rhythm Day, you will transfer money into it. Transfer it. Save it. It will add up. Using a strategy like this will make those one or two times per year when you have equipment needs painless.

THE POWER OF A GOOD QUESTION

In one of our weekly sales training meetings with our Incite Tax team members, we asked ourselves, "Why don't customers buy?"

We brainstormed a list. As a gym owner, I've seen many of these same reasons from our gym prospects too.

- Too expensive
- Just want an opinion (aka mooch)
- Don't like monthly "obligation" of payment
- Don't see/understand value
- Can do it themselves
- Don't trust or believe that the professional can do what they say

- Don't actually know what they want
- Want to avoid awkward firing of previous CPA
- Don't like change or are too lazy to make a change
- Not local enough

That's the first list we created and, to me, it seemed pretty complete. Then Ryan, our marketing director, whom I creatively like to call "our marketing guy," said, "That list is all about them. It's a list of blame toward the client."

Guess what blaming the client does for our business? Not a damn thing. It does not serve us to play the victim. It does not serve us to blame the prospect for not becoming a client. I can't take any action from that perspective. So we asked the next question: "Where are we at fault in these prospect excuses?"

Here is what we came up with.

- Too expensive—We failed to show them the value we offer.
- Just want an opinion (aka mooch)—While there will always be freeloaders, it doesn't do us any good to use this as an excuse. If I do a good enough job educating the prospect, even someone who originally just wanted an opinion could choose to work with us.
- Don't like monthly "obligation" of payment—We fail to be flexible to the clients' needs. Our tax firm should be more than happy to invoice the client only when they want us to do work instead of forcing them into a monthly payment that is easier for them to budget. For a gym, maybe your new member doesn't want to do group training. Maybe they just want personal training.
- Don't see/understand the value—We failed to educate and we failed to show value.
- Can do it themselves—We failed to show them why working with us is better for them. We failed to show them that they do one tax return a year and we do thousands. For a gym,

this could be the guy who looks as if he always skips leg day. "My way is doing me just fine, bro!"

- Don't trust or believe that the professional can do what they say—This could be us not showing enough confidence in ourselves to meet clients' needs or it could simply be we didn't build up enough credibility to earn the clients trust.
- They don't actually know what they want—We failed to guide them so they could determine through a conversation with us what they should want.
- Want to avoid awkward firing of previous CPA—If someone is blown away with what they will get from our services, this should never be an excuse. We clearly failed to show them the value of our services, and it could be we failed to guide them through how that process works. In real life it's super simple to switch CPAs.
- Don't like change or are too lazy to make a change—We failed to follow up with them. When a prospect leaves our office, guess what? They stop thinking about us. They could totally be sold on using us, but life happens.
- Not local—We failed to provide a good service. For an accounting firm, today's available technology makes distance a nonissue. We use Zoom to have face-to-face meetings. I think this may only be an issue for a gym if they move. Some existing members may not follow.

The right questions are so powerful, and you can see how the second set of questions gives us way better answers. It holds us accountable and empowers us to create our own action items to improve on these areas. Blaming the prospect for not hiring us gets us nowhere. It's way more effective acting like the captain[1] of our own ship instead of pretending to just be a passenger, because that is what happens when we make excuses instead of taking responsibility.

---

[1] William Ernest Henley, "Invictus," *Book of Verses* (1888)

Do you remember the list of excuses why a microgym isn't profitable? I'll re-share it so you don't have to flip back to Chapter 1.

- I'm ok that there is no money in this business because I'm serving a greater purpose.
- People are cheap and they won't pay my rates.
- It's really just a hobby I'm really passionate about. I don't even want to be paid.
- I just need ten more members.
- Numbers just aren't my thing. I'm not an accountant and I'll never understand this stuff.
- My members will think I'm greedy if they find out the gym is a very profitable business.
- There's no money in this business anyway.
- I'm just here to help people.

Committing to your Rhythm Days makes your gym immune to these types of excuses. It's how you take accountability for and act responsibility for the financial health and profitability of your gym.

BREAD AND BUTTER

My wife makes fun of me because, apparently, I had a neglected childhood. Why? Because my parents never taught me idioms, those common phrases that don't really make sense but have been endowed with a meaning we all accept. For example, bread and butter. As in, your Rhythm Days are the bread and butter of the Profit First system.

I like how Mike describes profit. "Profit is *not* an event. Profit is not something that happens at year-end or at the end of your five-year plan or someday. Profit isn't even something that waits until tomorrow. Profit must happen now and always. Profit must be baked into your business. Every day, every transaction, every moment. Profit is not an event. Profit is a habit."

Profit First for Microgyms is a set of guidelines designed to make gyms instantly profitable. It provides all the tools necessary to make that happen. It is a set of guidelines; you may choose to exclude some parts of it. For example, maybe you won't set up Remove Temptation accounts. Whatever parts you may choose to include or exclude, the Profit First system will not work for you if you aren't doing your Rhythm Days. The Rhythm Days are how you transform profit into a habit.

FINANCIAL WORKOUT

Are you committed to a profit habit? Of course you are! Determine and schedule your Rhythm Days. Commit to it. Do it.

You are busy. Things will come up and you will have so many opportunities to keep putting this off. Schedule your Rhythm Days so you know profit will happen.

This also means you are committing to not stressing out about paying bills. Choose where you will store your bills as they come in during the month, and only think about the bills when you sit down on your Rhythm Days.

CASH FLOW ANALYSIS

Y OU KNOW HOW THEY SAY THAT KIDS HAVE A BETTER CHANCE at success if they eat meals as a family? We try to do that. One particular dinner provided a great experience for us. In fact, it was such a great experience, it could have been a defining moment for our children, one that could have an impact on their future. It was one of those great experiences when you say to yourself, "I have failed as a parent." And, "Where did I go wrong?"

That night, my wife cooked chicken. Now, my kids have eaten chicken before. Most times, chicken is either a chicken breast or shredded chicken. This time, however, she cooked the whole chicken. She served what looked like a Thanksgiving turkey, just a lot smaller. Apparently, my kids have never seen a chicken with the bones still in it. It was as if my wife had cooked an alien! Had I known we would get such a wonderful reaction, I would have had my phone out to capture the looks on their faces.

"What is that!?!" they all said in eerily synchronized voices. Their faces had that look of disgust parents get when they first deal with a diaper blowout.

Throughout life, we all experience a lot of first times. It's perfectly natural if we have similar reactions to these new experiences, much as my kids did when they saw the alien chicken. At one time in his life, Bill Gates wrote code for the first time. Warren Buffet wasn't born making trades; he had a first time too. Rich Froning and Matt Fraser weren't born with the title "Fittest Man on Earth." Chris Cooper had to write his first blog post. Stu Brauer dropped his first F-bomb. I prepared my first tax return. There was a time you coached your first class. Maybe owning your microgym is the first time you've been a business owner. Your first time managing your cash flow might be right now.

The first time we do anything, most of us humans are terrible at it. Maybe you tried a cash flow management system once before and, since it was very new to you, you got frustrated and eventually gave up. Or maybe accounting and numbers aren't your thing and you're sure you'd suck at it, so you've never tried it.

If the only thing I accomplish by writing this book it is that you are willing to attempt to manage your cash flow, then this was a success. You deserve to be profitable, and the world needs you to spread the gift of health. Whether you have never tried a cash flow management system before, or you did try and it didn't go as planned, this book is for you. It's similar to when you are coaching a gym member to get a personal best. You see them fail on an attempt, but you know it's because their technique needs to be a little better. So, you give them a cue and you encourage them to try again. Wouldn't you know, they get it.

The first year I ran the Profit First system in my business, I sucked at it and I'm an accountant. I'm a Master Level Certified Profit First Professional. I deal with numbers and bank accounts all day, every day. I still sucked at it.

Please don't give up if you find that at first you are terrible at this. *Profit First for Microgyms* is giving you all the tools and resources you need to set you up for success. The system is thorough enough that it protects you from both rookie and expert mistakes that many make with their cash flow management.

Speaking of chicken, the Cash Flow Analysis you are learning in this chapter is kind of like the chicken and the egg debate. Which came first? Or which one should come first? Chickens are hatched from eggs, so naturally there was first an egg. However, eggs are created by chickens, so naturally the chicken came first. The Cash Flow Analysis, which is called the instant assessment in the original Profit First, is the start of figuring out how to manage your cash. It will give you a snapshot of the health of your business, like one of those famous "before and after" weight loss pictures.

Which came first, the Profit First principles or the Cash Flow Analysis? When I sat down to write this book, I wondered if I should start with the Cash Flow Analysis and then explain the principles or start with the principles first and then explain the Cash Flow Analysis. I went with the principles first because my hope is that now this analysis will make even more sense. That said, it isn't out of the realm of possibility that, after reading this chapter, rereading previous chapters may be even more enlightening.

In working with hundreds of microgyms, I have never once come across a gym owner who said they opened their gym because they wanted an excuse to do accounting and run cash flow reports all day. Please note, I did not say I've never once met a gym owner who is good at accounting. I know you have it within you to learn the skills you need as the CEO of your gym even if you aren't convinced yet. This may be the chapter that helps you see that.

We are going to get pretty technical as I walk you through how to fill out the Cash Flow Analysis for your gym, step by step. If the Rhythm Days are the bread and butter of *Profit First for Microgyms*, then the Cash Flow Analysis is the recipe that makes the bread. You have smaller plate bank accounts set up (your Essential Seven Accounts). You are taking the time to sit down and manage your cash by putting money into these new bank accounts. Now you may be wondering, how much money do you put in these accounts? And, what percentage of what number are you using to figure that out? By the end of this chapter, you'll have the answers to those questions.

A quick note, in *Profit First*, Mike called these an instant assessment. We are calling it a Cash Flow Analysis.

CAPS VS TAPS

As you do the steps in this chapter, you'll enter real data about your gym into the Cash Flow Analysis. You'll also identify your Current Allocation Percentages (CAPs), the percentage of your revenue that you allocate to your Essential Seven Accounts.

Occasionally, a gym owner tells us they can't possible have any CAPs yet because they haven't done this before. The Essential Seven Accounts exist in every gym all the time; the owners are just not aware of it. Nearly all pre-Profit First gym owners make the same mistake: They use one big plate, their business checking account. They've paid for team members before. They've purchased equipment before. The tax burden Uncle Sam throws in their faces has to be responded to each year. Profit First just makes us aware of these smaller plates. The Cash Flow Analysis will show you how you allocated funds in the past. (Don't worry; it's just a starting point.)

Another part of the analysis involves pulling a percentage from our *Profit First for Microgyms* table. In *Profit First*, Mike analyzed what healthy businesses were doing with their cash and created a table that shows a healthy business at their Real Revenue size and how they allocate to the different Profit First accounts. We are able to take Mike's original analysis even further to be specific to you. We looked at profitable microgyms and that's how we came up with the numbers for the *Profit First for Microgyms* table. When we get to that point, I will show you how to pull percentages from that table into your Cash Flow Analysis. Those percentages are called Target Allocation Percentages (TAPs). Think of CAPs as the "before" picture and TAPs as the "after" picture. TAPs are the long-term goal. They give you your first target to work toward. Each quarter, you will look at your CAPs and adjust them closer to the TAPs. We go over these adjustments in Chapter 12.

TIME TO WORK: COMPLETE YOUR CASH FLOW ANALYSIS

Before you start your gym's Cash Flow Analysis, grab the following:

1. Your profit and loss statement (P&L) from your last full year in business—not from your last twelve months of business, but your last full *calendar year* in business. For a Microgym, a calendar year of January through December is usually the best.

2. Your balance sheet from the same time period as your P&L. This will likely be a balance sheet as of December 31.
3. Tax returns for you and any business partners. Your partners may not want to share their tax returns with you. If that's the case, just ask them for their income tax rate.

TABLRE 8.1: CASH FLOW ANALYSIS						
	Actual	Actual %	TAP %	PF$	Compare	The Fix
Top Line Revenue	A1					
Cost of Items You Sell	A2					
Real Revenue	A3	B3 - 100%	C3 - 100%			
Team Members	A4	B4	C4	D4	E4	F4
Profit	A5	B5	C5	D5	E5	F5
Owner's Pay	A6	B6	C6	D6	E6	F6
Tax	A7	B7	C7	D7	E7	F7
Equipment	A8	B8	C8	D8	E8	F8
Operating Expenses	A9	B9	C9	D9	E9	F9

In table 8.1 we have labeled each box (or cell). Now I'll walk you through what you put in each cell. This is probably going to take you one to two hours to complete. There may be moments when you get frustrated. Just take a deep breath. You got this!

As you pull numbers from your P&L and balance sheet and enter them into the different boxes of this analysis, we encourage you to make a little mark on those documents so that when you look back at your statements, you can see if a number has already been entered. (This recommendation will definitely make more sense once you get to box A9. For now, just trust me.)

COLUMN A: ACTUAL

CASH FLOW ANALYSIS (A1)						
	Actual	Actual %	TAP %	PF$	Compare	The Fix
Top Line Revenue	$548,303					

A1: This is your Gross Revenue, the total amount of money you collected from your members for all services provided and all retail items sold. This is not the same thing as total deposits into your business bank accounts. If you took a loan that was deposited into your bank account, that is not part of Gross Revenue and doesn't go here. If you had to take money from your personal account to put into the business account to cover expenses, that is not Gross Revenue and doesn't go here. If you had an expense that was later refunded to you, that is not Gross Revenue. This box only represents total money collected from your members for services and products.

CASH FLOW ANALYSIS (A2)						
	Actual	Actual %	TAP %	PF$	Compare	The Fix
Top Line Revenue	$548,303					
Cost of Items You Sell	$15,425					

A2: In A1, you included the income made from selling retail items, such as hoodies, T-shirts, protein powder, cold-brewed coffee, and any supplements or branded apparel. In this cell you put how much you paid for those items. In the accounting world, this is often thought of as your cost of goods sold.

Rather than get really geeky on you by explaining how inventory works with accounting rules and how the tax rules on handling cost of goods sold has changed since the tax reform of 2018, I'll just say that you don't need to understand any of that to analyze your cash flow.

For this box, we have found it is easier and more logical to include any payments made for inventory (items you buy to later sell to others), even if the items haven't been sold yet. The first reason is, we are making sure that cash outflow will be captured here in our analysis.

The second reason is, it will help you realize that buying inventory can turn cash (in the financial world we use the term "liquid") into something that could sit on a shelf and gather dust. This also helps you see the power of taking preorders whenever possible. Sell the items before you spend your cash. We have seen a butt ton of financials from gym owners that show they bought inventory years ago with the high hopes of making money only to have those items sit in their gym for years. This doesn't mean you shouldn't have stock. Just be smart about it and don't hold on to inventory that may not sell.

CASH FLOW ANALYSIS (A3)						
	Actual	Actual %	TAP %	PF$	Compare	The Fix
Top Line Revenue	$548,303					
Cost of Items You Sell	$15,425					
Real Revenue	$532,878	B3 - 100%	C3 - 100%			

A3: This cell is just math. It's **A1 minus A2**, and that number is Real Revenue. See how easy this is? Ain't nothing gonna to slow you down!

CASH FLOW ANALYSIS (A4)						
	Actual	Actual %	TAP %	PF$	Compare	The Fix
Top Line Revenue	$548,303					
Cost of Items You Sell	$15,425					
Real Revenue	$532,878	B3 - 100%	C3 - 100%			
Team Members	$132,120	B4	C4	D4	E4	F4

A4: Now, add up what you paid your team members. If your coaches are independent contractors or employees or if you pay your coaches by the hour, or by a flat price per class, or by a percentage of the gym's income, or any combination of those pay structures, put that number here. If you have salaried team members who aren't coaches but handle front desk tasks or general manager functions or anything related to the operations of the gym, put that expense here. Whether you call them staff, employees, or team members, the gym's expense paying them goes in this box.

If you are coaching classes yourself, the portion of your pay that is directly related to coaching classes goes here too. We will get to the OWNER'S PAY box later. It's very easy to think of paying yourself for coaching classes as OWNER'S PAY because you as the owner are getting paid by the gym. However, we have a reason in separating your pay for coaching classes from your OWNER'S PAY category: If you don't think of coaching classes as a TEAM MEMBER expense, you will never know if you can hire another coach to replace you in classes. It's also easy for you and other microgym owners to think of coaching as part of your no-cost obligation to the gym. There *is* a cost to this, because if you were not part of the gym, the gym would need to pay someone else to coach that class.

CASH FLOW ANALYSIS (A5)						
	Actual	Actual %	TAP %	PF$	Compare	The Fix
Top Line Revenue	$548,303					
Cost of Items You Sell	$15,425					
Real Revenue	$532,878	B3 - 100%	C3 - 100%			
Team Members	$132,120	B4	C4	D4	E4	F4
Profit	$0.00	B5	C5	D5	E5	F5

A5: This box represents your profit, the cash left over after you collect from members and then pay the gym's expenses. Most microgym owners aren't consciously setting aside money to be distributed as a return on their investment. If you did, put that amount here. Setting aside profit is not the only way profit can show up. You could have profit in two other ways that are easy to overlook.

Include the change in your bank balances from last year. For example, if you had $10,000 in the bank at the start of the year and at the end of the year you had $13,000 in the bank, you'd have a $3,000 increase, which you would include in the number that goes in this box. (Your balance sheet should show this information.) On the flip side, if your balance went from $10,000 to $7,000, a $3,000 decrease, then that negative number is included in the number that goes here in the profit cell.

What if you took out loans during the year? That is cash coming in, and this is the place to note that. However, you'll have to add it as a negative number. The reason is, the loan deposit was not included in box A1 (Gross Revenue), and it doesn't make sense to put the loan in any of the other A-column boxes. Yet, the loan deposit is still cash flow and it needs to be accounted for in our analysis. On the other hand, if you are paying down loan balances, your ability to do that is coming from your profit. So you would add that positive number here. For example, if I had a loan of $10,000 at the beginning of the year, but by the end of the year the loan balance is now $7,000. I would add $3,000 to my profit box.

Credit card balances and any other debt is treated the same way. If the balance of the credit cards or debt increases, then I need to put that negative number here in the profit cell. If the balances go down, then I put that in as a positive number.

Mike made an important point about this box in *Profit First*. "This is the cumulative profit you have sitting in the bank or have distributed to yourself (and/or partners) as a bonus on top of—but not to supplement—your salary. If you think you have a profit, but it is not in the bank and was never distributed to you as a bonus, this means you don't really have a profit."

CASH FLOW ANALYSIS (A6)						
	Actual	Actual %	TAP %	PF$	Compare	The Fix
Top Line Revenue	$548,303					
Cost of Items You Sell	$15,425					
Real Revenue	$532,878	B3 - 100%	C3 - 100%			
Team Members	$132,120	B4	C4	D4	E4	F4
Profit	$0.00	B5	C5	D5	E5	F5
Owner's Pay	$133,799	B6	C6	D6	E6	F6

A6: OWNER'S PAY is any cash outflow from the business that supports your lifestyle. It will include any W-2 pay or monthly distributions taken by you to cover your monthly personal expenses. As to the W-2 pay, it only includes the amount that hits your personal account. What do I mean? If my gross W-2 amount is $5,000 per month, that is not the amount of income that is deposited into my personal account. The most I would see is $4,617.50 because I have a payroll tax burden the government forces me to voluntarily pay. Since I want to be super accurate on this, I am only going to count $4,617.50 or whatever dollar amount hits my personal account as OWNER'S PAY. The rest will be captured in cell A9 under OPERATING EXPENSE. You don't really have to do any math or crazy accounting crap to figure this out. It's the dollar amount of the check or, if you have direct deposit, it's the dollar amount that hits your personal account.

Your W-2 is not the only number we consider here. We also need to consider distributions. If you are working with a decent tax professional—they don't even have to be excellent the way we are at Incite Tax, just decent—they will at least have you in a tax structure in which part of your monthly pay is a W-2 and part of your monthly pay is considered an owner distribution, or owner's draw, or shareholder distribution. (For accounting purposes, those three terms all mean the same thing.)

We also need to ask the question, if you were not the owner of the gym, what expenses would the gym *not* have? Is there a simpler way to ask that question? Meh. I don't know. So let me provide some examples. Does my gym need me to have a cell phone to operate? Maybe. If I were not an owner of the gym, would the gym cover my cell phone bill? Not likely. So, while this is a likely tax write-off, it is much more an OWNER'S PAY expense then it is an operating expense.

Or let's say I decide to travel to California to interview, brainstorm, and get some mentoring advice from a fellow microgym owner. After setting up the business trip, I decide to visit some family members that live in the area and spend a day at Disneyland. Assuming I follow the tax rules for business travel, the gym would pay for my travel expenses, such as airfare and hotel fees for this trip. Is that expense really needed to keep my doors open? Maybe. If I were not the owner of the gym, would it pay for my travel expenses for this? Not likely. That would also be consider an OWNER'S PAY amount.

Any expense that our gym pays for that we can take as a tax deduction but would likely not be covered by a gym if we were not the owner is considered OWNER'S PAY and that number will be placed in this box.

This is one of my favorite accounts because, of all the Essential Seven Accounts, it's the largest cash benefit to you and if you've found yourself feeling depressed about not having anything to show for your hard work, this lets you see the benefits you're receiving that are not directly through a W-2 or owner distribution.

This expense benefit does add complexity that if you're not aware of it, will screw up your allocation days. Let me explain the situation that may arise. Let's pretend the OWNER'S PAY allocation is $3,000. Before transferring the $3,000 from the INCOME account to the OWNER'S PAY account, you need to look at the expenses that were paid out of the OPEX account that are really considered OWNER'S PAY. If you don't, then you end up paying yourself more than your CAP. Let's pretend the cell phone bill was paid for $100 and gas for your car cost $50. So instead of transferring $3,000, you would only transfer $2,850 because you already got the OWNER'S PAY benefit of the $150 that was expensed.

CASH FLOW ANALYSIS (A7)						
	Actual	Actual %	TAP %	PF$	Compare	The Fix
Top Line Revenue	$548,303					
Cost of Items You Sell	$15,425					
Real Revenue	$532,878	B3 - 100%	C3 - 100%			
Team Members	$132,120	B4	C4	D4	E4	F4
Profit	$0.00	B5	C5	D5	E5	F5
Owner's Pay	$133,799	B6	C6	D6	E6	F6
Tax	$0.00	B7	C7	D7	E7	F7

A7: Now we have the tax line. This is the money set aside to cover the income tax burden the business is generating that you'll end up paying on your personal tax return. This is super critical because, under Profit First, we don't want you to have to dip into OWNER'S PAY, which is supporting your lifestyle, in order to cover the income tax burden. We believe that the business and its profit is generating the tax burden so the business should have to pay that tax burden, not you. If my take-home, OWNER'S PAY amount is $5,000, with Profit First, I will be using all $5,000 of that for my lifestyle. I will not be setting aside any of that $5,000 to cover my income tax. That's why we have this account. The gym is going to set the money aside. In this way, Profit First is a way to get the gym to serve your life rather than you serving the gym.

It's important to note that this is just for income taxes. Payroll taxes and sales taxes are part of operating expenses. That's a tax the business has to pay.

Also, don't feel bad if the gym has never set aside money for you to cover your personal income tax burden. It's super-duper really extremely rare that a gym owner does this if they haven't learned the Profit First system. Your number may be zero now, and that is fine. We all start somewhere. I started at zero too.

CASH FLOW ANALYSIS (A8)						
	Actual	Actual %	TAP %	PF$	Compare	The Fix
Top Line Revenue	$548,303					
Cost of Items You Sell	$15,425					
Real Revenue	$532,878	B3 - 100%	C3 - 100%			
Team Members	$132,120	B4	C4	D4	E4	F4
Profit	$0.00	B5	C5	D5	E5	F5
Owner's Pay	$133,799	B6	C6	D6	E6	F6
Tax	$0.00	B7	C7	D7	E7	F7
Equipment	$5,578.42	B8	C8	D8	E8	F8

A8: This is the equipment box and it covers small equipment to big equipment and every size in between. You may have an expense item on your P&L titled something like Small Equipment or Small Tools. This will include the amounts that are likely showing up on your balance sheet under fixed assets. This box is not for equipment such as computer or furniture. It's gym equipment: dumbbells, kettlebells, barbells, weight plates, Torpedos, plyo boxes, medicine balls, bands, jump ropes, boxing gloves, punching bags, yoga mats, ab mats, bikes, InBodys, rowers, rigs, rings—those types of things.

You will also include any equipment repair or maintenance expenses. On your P&L, this is probably under the category Repairs and Maintenance. Just double check that you are only including expenses related to equipment repair and maintenance. Our firm has seen other types of expenses like cleaning under that category as well. Cleaning is not a number you include in this box. By the time you've added up the total for this box, the number should represent how much you spent to add, replace, and maintain the equipment you use to provide your services.

CASH FLOW ANALYSIS (A9)						
	Actual	Actual %	TAP %	PF$	Compare	The Fix
Top Line Revenue	$548,303					
Cost of Items You Sell	$15,425					
Real Revenue	$532,878	B3 - 100%	C3 - 100%			
Team Members	$132,120	B4	C4	D4	E4	F4
Profit	$0	B5	C5	D5	E5	F5
Owner's Pay	$133,799	B6	C6	D6	E6	F6
Tax	$0	B7	C7	D7	E7	F7
Equipment	$5,578.42	B8	C8	D8	E8	F8
Operating Expenses	$258,316	B9	C9	D9	E9	F9

A9: This bottom box represents your operating expenses. Basically, all the other cash outflows we haven't already identified go in this box. Please be patient with yourself on this box. It's the most complicated one. After you are finished with this box, you will fly through the rest of the boxes. This one can be a little trickier to add up because it isn't as simple as taking the total expenses from your P&L. You have to make sure you don't double count other cash outflows that you already identified from the previous cells. Remember when I asked you to put a mark next to the line items you already noted on your financials? This is exactly why that tip is helpful.

Our recommended approach is to start with Total Expenses, which can be found at the bottom of all of the numbers on your P&L right before Net Income. That is our starting number for this calculation.

Next, look at the section of your P&L called Costs of Goods Sold. This section probably includes your costs for the items you resell, such as apparel and supplements. As mentioned in our explanation of box A2, we should have already accounted for our cost of retail sales. In addition though, there may be some other cash outflows that are in this section. These numbers are not actually part of "total expenses" on your P&L, so we want to make sure we add any other expenses that are in the Cost of Goods Sold section that we haven't put in any of the previous boxes. This is *another* reason why I recommend making a mark next to the items you have included in boxes A1 through A8.

You should now have your Total Expenses plus any remaining items you were showing under the Cost of Goods Sold section that were not previously included. Now you want to look at the expense section of your P&L statement, which lists all the expenses. This bottom section is part of the Total Expenses. This means you'll have to subtract the numbers you have already included in boxes A1 through A8. That way we aren't double counting those cash outflows. This should be easy to see if you made the marks on the P&L as you were going along. As an example, your W-2 amounts would be in this section and you already put that under OWNER'S PAY. You have to do this for every single number you have already included in the previous boxes. Table 8.2 gives an example of what your calculation may look like.

Notice how all the expenses in my example have been included in previous boxes. Doing this allows you to get to the true operating expenses for your gym.

For our Cash Flow Analysis, this box is going to be total expenses plus any cost of goods sold not already included, and minus the other expenses already included in A1 through A8. Please note that you are only looking at the P&L to figure out this number, because the balance sheet items are not part of the Total Expense number you started with.

Congrats, you are now finished with the A boxes and the most time-consuming part of the Cash Flow Analysis. The rest is simple math and pulling numbers from the *Profit First for Microgyms* table. Filling out column A is about 80 percent of the work when doing a Cash Flow Analysis. The hardest part is now in the rearview mirror.

TABLE 8.2: OPERATING EXPENSE DETAIL	
Total Expenses	$463,138.00
Coach Expense	-$186,055.00
Equipment	-$5,578.00
W-2 Amount	-$32,000.00
Cell Phone	-$1,200.00
Travel	-$145.00
Car Payments & Gas	-$6,520.00
Eating Out	-$1,674.00
Health Insurance	-$1,481.00
401K Fees	-$9,104.00
Corporate Rent Strategy	-$15,000.00
Operating Expenses	$204,381.00

COLUMN B: ACTUAL % OF REAL REVENUE

CASH FLOW ANALYSIS (B3-9)						
	Actual	Actual %	TAP %	PF$	Compare	The Fix
Top Line Revenue	$548,303					
Cost of Items You Sell	$15,425					
Real Revenue	$532,878	100%	C3 - 100%			
Team Members	$132,120	25%	C4	D4	E4	F4
Profit	$0	0%	C5	D5	E5	F5
Owner's Pay	$133,799	25%	C6	D6	E6	F6
Tax	$0	0%	C7	D7	E7	F7
Equipment	$5,578.42	1%	C8	D8	E8	F8
Operating Expenses	$258,316	48%	C9	D9	E9	F9

B3: This box is always 100%. Yes, B1 and B2 are left blank. The B column is all about math and luckily, simple math at that. You'll be able to do this section really fast.

B4: This cell is **A4 divided by A3**. This shows you what percentage of your Real Revenue TEAM MEMBER expense was for your gym.

B5: This box is **A5 divided by A3**. This shows you how much of your Real Revenue you were able to keep as PROFIT.

B6: This box is **A6 divided by A3**. (You may be seeing the pattern by now). This shows you how much of your Real Revenue you were able to take as OWNER'S PAY.

B7: This box is **A7 divided by A3**. You guessed it: this shows you how much of your Real Revenue your business paid to cover your personal income TAX burden.

B8: I probably don't really need to keep giving you the formula, but for the sake of consistency, I will. This box is **A8 divided by A3** and represents how much of your Real Revenue you used for EQUIPMENT needs.

B9: This box is **A9 divided by A3** which shows you how much Real Revenue you used to operate the gym (your OPEX account).

COLUMN C: FINANCIALLY FIT %

CASH FLOW ANALYSIS (C3-9)						
	Actual	Actual %	TAP %	PF$	Compare	The Fix
Top Line Revenue	$548,303					
Cost of Items You Sell	$15,425					
Real Revenue	$532,878	100%	100%			
Team Members	$132,120	25%	25%	D4	E4	F4
Profit	$0	0%	10%	D5	E5	F5
Owner's Pay	$133,799	25%	15%	D6	E6	F6
Tax	$0	0%	10%	D7	E7	F7
Equipment	$5,578.42	1%	5%	D8	E8	F8
Operating Expenses	$258,316	48%	35%	D9	E9	F9

The C column is all about the *Profit First for Microgyms* percentages in table 8.3. You pull the percentages from the table and insert them here into your Cash Flow Analysis. C1 and C2 will be left blank and C3, just like B3, is always 100%.

TABLE 8.3			
Real Rev Range (up to)			
	$300,000	$650,000	$1,000,000
Real Revenue	100%	100%	100%
Team Members	25%	25%	25%
Profit	5%	10%	15%
Owner's Pay	15%	15%	15%
Tax	5%	10%	10%
Equipment	5%	5%	5%
Operating Expenses	45%	35%	30%

If your Real Revenue is less than $300,000 then take the percentages in the first column and plug them into the C column. If your Real Revenue is less than $650,000 but more than $300,000, then use the second column. If your Real Revenue is more than $650,000, then use the third column.

The only box I want to specifically address is C4. If you did things the right way, then the number in box C4 should be 25%. In our research, 25% is what the most financially fit gyms are doing. However, we know from experience that 44% is also pretty good. So if your percentage in B5 is so far off and 25% seems impossible, then you may adjust the C4 percentage to 44%.

COLUMN D: TARGET DOLLAR AMOUNTS

The D column becomes another math column. This whole column is going to show you what a financially fit microgym with your exact Real Revenue would be allocating to their Essential Seven Accounts. Leave D1, D2, and D3 blank.

CASH FLOW ANALYSIS (D4–9)						
	Actual	Actual %	TAP %	PF$	Compare	The Fix
Top Line Revenue	$548,303					
Cost of Items You Sell	$15,425					
Real Revenue	$532,878	100%	100%			
Team Members	$132,120	25%	25%	$133,219.50	E4	F4
Profit	$0	0%	10%	$53,287.80	E5	F5
Owner's Pay	$133,799	25%	15%	$79,931.70	E6	F6
Tax	$0	0%	10%	$53,287.80	E7	F7
Equipment	$5,578.42	1%	5%	$26,643.90	E8	F8
Operating Expenses	$258,316	48%	35%	$186,507.30	E9	F9

D4: This is **A4 multiplied by C4**.
D5: This is **A5 multiplied by C5**.
D6: This is **A6 multiplied by C6**.
D7: This is **A7 multiplied by C7**.
D8: This is **A8 multiplied by C8**.
D9: This is **A9 multiplied by C9**.

COLUMNS E AND F: COMPARE IT, THEN FIX IT

The E and F columns are all about comparison. You'll see how you compare to financially fit gyms that have similar Revenue. E1, E2, and E3 are also going to be blank. The math for column E is simple. Column F is where you put the action to take. Column F won't be as easy as the simple math you've been doing, but it isn't going to be that difficult for you.

CASH FLOW ANALYSIS (E4)						
	Actual	Actual %	TAP %	PF$	Compare	The Fix
Top Line Revenue	$548,303					
Cost of Items You Sell	$15,425					
Real Revenue	$532,878	100%	100%			
Team Members	$132,120	25%	25%	$133,219.50	–$1,099.50	Sweet
Profit	$0	0%	10%	$53,287.80	E5	F5
Owner's Pay	$133,799	25%	15%	$79,931.70	E6	F6
Tax	$0	0%	10%	$53,287.80	E7	F7
Equipment	$5,578.42	1%	5%	$26,643.90	E8	F8
Operating Expenses	$258,316	48%	35%	$186,507.30	E9	F9

E4: A4 minus D4. If the number is a positive number, then in F4 add the word "decrease." As in, we need to figure out how to get that expense down. A positive number here means that you are spending a higher percentage of your Real Revenue on your team members than a financially fit gym.

If the number is negative, then put "sweet" in F4. A negative number means that you are spending a smaller percentage of your Real Revenue here than our financially fit gyms. While this scenario is the opposite of having a positive number in E4, your action is not to "increase." I am not going to encourage you to spend more money on team members if your current level of spending is providing a great member experience already. I am also not going to encourage you to spend more on team members if your team members are currently getting a fair rate for their services.

Now, if your team members aren't getting a fair rate, and/or you know that they are loyal to you and that they have been willing to take a lower pay to help out your gym, a negative number in E4 means you have room to increase their pay.

Here's the last note for this box. If you are coaching classes, your pay for that service is included in this number. The number may be negative because you haven't been paying yourself for coaching classes. Stop doing that. If you have been doing that, then the negative number represents how much cash you could use to replace some of your own coaching blocks.

CASH FLOW ANALYSIS (E5)						
	Actual	Actual %	TAP %	PF$	Compare	The Fix
Top Line Revenue	$548,303					
Cost of Items You Sell	$15,425					
Real Revenue	$532,878	100%	100%			
Team Members	$132,120	25%	25%	$133,219.50	–$1,099.50	Sweet
Profit	$0	0%	10%	$53,287.80	–$53,287.80	Increase
Owner's Pay	$133,799	25%	15%	$79,931.70	E6	F6
Tax	$0	0%	10%	$53,287.80	E7	F7
Equipment	$5,578.42	1%	5%	$26,643.90	E8	F8
Operating Expenses	$258,316	48%	35%	$186,507.30	E9	F9

E5: A5 minus D5. If this is a negative number, then put "increase" in F5. This means that fit gyms are paying a higher percentage of their Real Revenue in Profit.

If this number is a positive number, then in F5 put "evaluate." A positive number here means that you are paying a higher amount of your Real Revenue in Profit than our financially fit gyms. This could be a good thing or a bad thing or it could be just a simple adjustment thing.

If your other actual numbers end up being "in-line" with or better than the fit gym numbers, then a positive number here is a good thing and there is no need to change anything.

If some numbers need to be adjusted, then a positive number here means that you have room to fix those numbers by simply reducing the cash you take for profit and adding it to the other areas that need to be increased.

If E5 is positive, and your take-home pay number in E6 is positive, that means you are probably paying yourself sporadically and unpredictably. A positive number here means you can fix that situation. You can decrease what you are taking as profit and increase the amount of OWNER'S PAY, which is going to be paid out at least monthly. Now you can have a stable OWNER'S PAY take-home amount.

CASH FLOW ANALYSIS (E6)						
	Actual	Actual %	TAP %	PF$	Compare	The Fix
Top Line Revenue	$548,303					
Cost of Items You Sell	$15,425					
Real Revenue	$532,878	100%	100%			
Team Members	$132,120	25%	25%	$133,219.50	–$1,099.50	Sweet
Profit	$0	0%	10%	$53,287.80	–$53,287.80	Increase
Owner's Pay	$133,799	25%	15%	$79,931.70	$53,867.30	Evaluate
Tax	$0	0%	10%	$53,287.80	E7	F7
Equipment	$5,578.42	1%	5%	$26,643.90	E8	F8
Operating Expenses	$258,316	48%	35%	$186,507.30	E9	F9

E6: A6 minus D6. If this is a negative number, then put "increase" in F6. This means that financially fit gyms are paying a higher percentage of their Real Revenue in OWNER'S PAY than you are.

If this number is a positive number, then put "evaluate." A positive number here means that you are paying a higher amount of your Real Revenue in OWNER'S PAY than the fit gyms. As was the case with your PROFIT account analysis from F5, you need to figure out if this is a good thing, bad thing, or just a thing.

If your other actual numbers end up being "in-line" with or better than the financially fit gyms, then a positive number here is a good thing and there is no need to change anything.

If some of the other numbers need to be fixed, then a positive number here means that you have room to fix those numbers by simply adjusting your OWNER'S PAY.

Well, maybe not so simply. In Chapter 5, I showed you how to figure out your minimum OWNER'S PAY. If the bare minimum you currently need is more than a financially fit gym is paying, then the adjustment that is needed may not be found here on this Cash Flow Analysis. It's possible that you need to look harder at what your gym can afford to pay you. It's also possible that your lifestyle is more expensive than the gym can afford. I'm not trying to make light of that or minimize how difficult looking at that situation can be. If you are serious about the financial health of your gym, looking at the cost of running your life is something that has to be addressed.

Note in the example that the E6 number is positive so we put "evaluate." You can see that we aren't taking enough from the PROFIT account and so would ultimately decide to decrease OWNER'S PAY and increase the PROFIT and TAX accounts.

CASH FLOW ANALYSIS (E7)						
	Actual	Actual %	TAP %	PF$	Compare	The Fix
Top Line Revenue	$548,303					
Cost of Items You Sell	$15,425					
Real Revenue	$532,878	100%	100%			
Team Members	$132,120	25%	25%	$133,219.50	–$1,099.50	Sweet
Profit	$0	0%	10%	$53,287.80	–$53,287.80	Increase
Owner's Pay	$133,799	25%	15%	$79,931.70	$53,867.30	Evaluate
Tax	$0	0%	10%	$53,287.80	–$53,287.80	Increase
Equipment	$5,578.42	1%	5%	$26,643.90	E8	F8
Operating Expenses	$258,316	48%	35%	$186,507.30	E9	F9

E7: A7 minus D7. If this number is a negative number, then put "increase" in F7. This means that our financially fit gyms are saving a higher percentage of Real Revenue to cover the owner's tax burden then you currently are.

If the number is positive it means you could put "decrease" in F7. However, let me give you some behind the scenes info that I think will help you make a better decision. We have adjusted the *Profit First Microgym* table from the original *Profit First* table, and the discussion I had with Mike about the tax percentages was an interesting one. You see, the original table suggests saving 15% of your Real Revenue for taxes, which you can see is not what I am recommending.

I have always felt, as a tax genius (self-proclaimed maybe, but I really do think we are awesome at it), that 15% was ridiculously high. Once I became a Mastery Level Certified Profit First Professional and was running Cash Flow Analysis on businesses, in many cases, if a business had to save 15% of their Real Revenue for taxes, it meant they were paying way more than their legal fair share. It means they either didn't have a tax genius in their corner to guide them, or their tax guy was terrible, worthless, and possibly an undercover IRS agent. So, I asked Mike about it. His main reason in suggesting such a high percentage was because of all the areas of cash flow management, the one that if mismanaged could carry some pretty dire consequences is not having the money to pay the tax man. Frankly, there's some risk with even suggesting what you should be saving for taxes. If I suggest something too low, now I could be the one to blame if you don't have enough cash to pay your tax burden. At 15%, the chance of suggesting too low a number becomes really, really, really, really small. Not eliminated of course, just tiny, tiny, tiny.

If you know you might feel anxious about not saving enough for taxes, then err on the side of a higher percentage here. After all, if you over-save for taxes, you can always take what's left and do something with it. This was the case with Matt Titus, the owner of Blackbird CrossFit. After paying his tax bill, he had a good chunk of change left. He used 85% of this leftover money to pay off a high interest credit card and applied the remaining 15% toward improving his physical gym space.

CASH FLOW ANALYSIS (E8)						
	Actual	Actual %	TAP %	PF$	Compare	The Fix
Top Line Revenue	$548,303					
Cost of Items You Sell	$15,425					
Real Revenue	$532,878	100%	100%			
Team Members	$132,120	25%	25%	$133,219.50	–$1,099.50	Sweet
Profit	$0	0%	10%	$53,287.80	–$53,287.80	Increase
Owner's Pay	$133,799	25%	15%	$79,931.70	$53,867.30	Evaluate
Tax	$0	0%	10%	$53,287.80	–$53,287.80	Increase
Equipment	$5,578.42	1%	5%	$26,643.90	–$21,065.48	Increase
Operating Expenses	$258,316	48%	35%	$186,507.30	E9	F9

E8: A8 minus D8. A negative number here means you aren't spending as much on equipment compared to financially fit gyms. Go ahead and put an "increase" in F8, and let me explain that, if you've felt strapped for cash, I'm not surprised that E8 is a negative number. I get it. In the early months of being an owner of CrossFit GSL, we only spent money on equipment when we absolutely had to. That also meant though that we were using the "hope and pray" method of cash flow management. We really hoped that we'd have no major equipment breakdown, because, if we did, we had no idea how the gym would pay for a replacement. Likely, we wouldn't have been able to afford it.

A positive number in E8 means you can put a "decrease" in F8. The good news if you fall into this situation is that you likely don't need to be spending as much as you are on equipment. If you are in this scenario, you probably have a gigantic heart and/or an extreme attraction to shiny new objects. We all want our members to have the best experience possible. New equipment is one of the ways we try to improve their experience. I am just suggesting that if you are spending more on equipment than our financially fit gyms, then you probably aren't adding as much to your members' experience as you may have thought.

When it comes to equipment being a specific focus in Profit First, it isn't about what you have or haven't done in the past. It's a little about *spending* the right amount and more about *saving* the right amount.

Some years you likely won't have heavy cash outflow on equipment and repairs. Other years your cash outflow could be a butt ton. By saving a percentage of your Real Revenue for equipment, you will be able to even out the cash burden of fluctuating equipment needs.

CASH FLOW ANALYSIS (E9)						
	Actual	Actual %	TAP %	PF$	Compare	The Fix
Top Line Revenue	$548,303					
Cost of Items You Sell	$15,425					
Real Revenue	$532,878	100%	100%			
Team Members	$132,120	25%	25%	$133,219.50	–$1,099.50	Sweet
Profit	$0	0%	10%	$53,287.80	–$53,287.80	Increase
Owner's Pay	$133,799	25%	15%	$79,931.70	$53,867.30	Evaluate
Tax	$0	0%	10%	$53,287.80	–$53,287.80	Increase
Equipment	$5,578.42	1%	5%	$26,643.90	–$21,065.48	Increase
Operating Expenses	$258,316	48%	35%	$186,507.30	$71,808.70	Decrease

E9: A9 minus D9. A negative number here means you aren't spending as much on operating expenses as our financially fit gyms. You could put "increase" in F9, but I'm not going to say that is the only solution. After all, if you spend less on operating expenses than the gyms we looked at for our Profit First for Microgyms table, then you could be one of these financially fit gyms already, which means that you are able to take higher profits or higher OWNER'S PAY. So you could put "no change needed" in F9 if you want.

A positive number, on the other hand, means you are spending more than our fit gyms. So put "decrease" in F9. Many microgyms find themselves in this situation. Yet again, it's more evidence of Parkinson's law. It's only natural to spend money out of your account if it's the only one you have, if it's just a large plate. With a new Profit First focus, you can now be more purposeful in handling your operating expenses.

BRAND NEW GYMS

A common question Mike gets when he presents on Profit First is how this can apply to new businesses. He explained this in *Profit First:*

> How does Profit First work if you just launched your business and have no revenue? Should you wait until you have some to start using Profit First? Heck, no. Starting with squat, with your whole business future ahead of you is actually the best time to start using Profit First. Why? Because it allows you to form a powerful habit right from the getgo, when your business is forming and, perhaps more important, prevents you from developing bad financial habits that can be difficult to break.
>
> "Also, in the early stages of building a business, you need to spend as much time as possible on the selling and the doing; systems and processes come later. For these reasons, it's best not to worry about getting the exact right percentages for your business. Simply use the percentages in the [Cash Flow Analysis] for your target allocations, but start at 1 percent allocation for the PROFIT account, 50 percent for [OWNER'S PAY], and 15 percent for the TAX account. Use quarterly adjustments to step up to higher percentages and nudge your business closer to the TAPs recommended in this book. The goal for new businesses is to form the basic core of the Profit First good habit and then spend every other waking second getting your baby off the ground.

For your gym, you are just going to slightly tweak Mike's advice. He called it an instant assessment. We call it a Cash Flow Analysis. Rather than use generic business percentages, use the ones that have been adjusted for the microgym industry—except for the profit account which should stay at Mike's suggested 1%. Why? Because the point is establishing the habit of setting aside money for profit. We also recommend keeping your equipment cost at 1%. Because you are a brand new gym, the existing equipment or your new equipment should last for at least a year.

The last tweak is related to TEAM MEMBER expense. If you will be the only one coaching the classes in the beginning, then you pay yourself as you would a coach. If you were going to pay a coach $20 to teach the class, and you are the one who teaches it, you pay yourself that $20. On top of that, you will also pay yourself the OWNER'S PAY percentage.

NEED MORE HELP?

As promised, this chapter was very technical. It's a lot. I get it. So, in an effort to serve you even more, we have a free challenge we put together. Go to www.ProfitFirstForMicrogyms.com/5days. It breaks down doing the Cash Flow Analysis steps into five days. Each day is designed to take no more than fifteen minutes. After the five days, you have a completed Cash Flow Analysis. It also happens to be free. I mean *really and truly* free. It's not like one of those things where you answer a bunch of questions and before you get to the results, they tell you in order to see the results you need to pay money. It's really completely free. You just need to be willing to invest your time.

Now if that isn't your workout of choice, but you still think you need a little more help, I created a video walking through an example of filling out the Cash Flow Analysis. I show you the financial statements I'm using and where I'm pulling the numbers from as I put them in the analysis. You can find this video at www.ProfitFirstForMicrogyms.com/tools.

FINANCIAL WORKOUT

Do it! Block out time on your calendar right now and schedule this. Make time to do your Cash Flow Analysis. Every journey begins with a starting point. This is yours.

Since I know you already scheduled your Rhythm Days, you basically gave yourself a deadline on when you need to get this analysis done. You need to know your CAPs to have a successful Rhythm Day. So channel your inner Rob Schneider from *Waterboy*. "You can do eet!"

CHAPTER 9

THE LANGUAGE OF BUSINESS

L ANGUAGE IN ITS SIMPLEST FORM IS JUST A SYSTEM OF communicating with a group of people. If you are in Mexico, you need to speak Spanish. In France, it's French. Germany; German. We often think of language in the form of words, but it is more than that.

Before I moved to Argentina, I was told I would have to learn Spanish in order to communicate with the Argentineans. Even though I got As in Spanish in high school, I admit that I learned nothing. So, I spent three months cramming so I could learn how to speak Spanish.

With my useless two years of high school Spanish and three months of intense focus, I got on a plane headed for Buenos Aires. I was confident that I could hold a conversation. My seat neighbor was from Argentina and he was a chatterbox. I introduced myself to him using my newly acquired Spanish skills. "Mi nombre es John Briggs. Como està?"

About two seconds into the conversation I had exhausted my entire skill set, everything I had learned over the last three months. The next thirteen (THIRTEEN!) hours was a whirlwind. My seat neighbor spoke much faster than the videos and recordings I had studied. He most definitely used words I had never heard. My mind raced with bad translations and my own thoughts. Did he just say something about a chocolate whale? Or a spider that shines lights? Please let him stop talking. I'm in so far over my head. How long can I fake this smile and just shake my head like an idiot? Do you think he can tell I have no idea what he is talking about? I desperately needed a translator to interpret his words and communicate them to me in a way that I would understand them.

As it turned out, I had learned the wrong language. When I arrived in Buenos Aires, Argentineans quickly corrected me and informed me that they speak Castellano. For someone who finds conflict slightly uncomfortable, I for sure was not one to argue with an entire country. Of course in my mind, Castellano is 99% Spanish words, the same words I could use if I were traveling to Mexico. To Argentineans, though, Castellano is much more than words. It's the accent used and the intonation of sentences. It was a system of communication and words were just part of it.

When traveling to foreign countries, you'll certainly have the best experience if you know their language. If that isn't possible, getting a translator could be the next best thing. When traveling around the world of business, you'll have the best experience if you understand its language: accounting. If you didn't spend your college years getting an accounting degree, the next best thing to understanding accounting is to have a translator. Maybe you're thinking this friggin' amazing book has sometimes seemed like a foreign language, and maybe the last chapter doing the Cash Flow Analysis has left you with a feeling of jetlag. It will all be worth it! You are going to find profitability. You deserve it! Profit First translates the past confusion of financial topics into a clear language that's easy to understand.

Have you ever searched Google for "translation fails"? If you do, you will be provided with some really hilarious examples of not understanding a language. As you scroll through the results, you won't find a single example of translation fails that relate to the language of accounting. Let's be real though, translation fails can and do happen when it comes to accounting, and the situations aren't always going to be as funny as an Arabic bathroom sign with an English translation that reads: "Toilet—The Place of Prayer."

In this chapter, we'll review two translation tools that are part of the Profit First system. These tools will help you translate your numbers into action. Before we get into that, though, we need to talk about quality bookkeeping—or the lack thereof.

THE IMPORTANCE OF QUALITY BOOKKEEPING

Profit First is an amazing system with super powerful tools that will help you assess the current health of your business and help you become healthier and profitable. However, the system doesn't replace your bookkeeping. That still has to get done. Further, Profit First can only be as useful as the quality of your bookkeeping. Before we do the Cash Flow Analysis for our Incite Tax clients and dig into these translation tools, we take the time to thoroughly review the client's books.

We start with the basics, making sure all of the accounts—bank, credit cards, and liabilities—have been reconciled to their statements. Reconciling is a process of matching the transactions that are in your real accounts by looking at the statements and confirming the transactions have been entered in the accounting software. If all the accounts reconcile correctly, then the ending balances in the accounting software match the ending balances from the statements. More importantly, you know all the transactions are at least in the software, meaning there aren't missing transactions or extra transactions.

Confirming the accounts are reconciled, we now check to see if the transactions have been categorized correctly and consistently. If I am using Mindbody for my gym management, I want to make sure I categorize that expense the same way every month. You could call it dues and subscriptions, or software, or something else; just make sure it's the same category every month. We check that with everything. Most accounting software allows you to run a report so that you can see all the transactions, something like a transaction by detail report. We export that report to Excel and then we can sort it by the vendor's name to quickly see if the payments to each vendor have consistent categorization.

Then, we review deposits to make sure only income transactions are hitting that category. Sometimes deposits can be mistakenly categorized as income, such as owner contributions or refunds from vendors.

Once we have confidence in the quality of the bookkeeping, we can trust the information we use not only in the Cash Flow Analysis but also in these translation tools.

If you would like more help on bookkeeping, our resource page at www.ProfitFirstForMicrogyms.com/tools has a training that goes over the basics of a bookkeeping system.

THE TWO TYPES OF EXPENSES THAT REALLY MATTER

Whether your Cash Flow Analysis shows your operating expenses are in line with a financially fit gym or it shows you have a whole lot of expenses to cut, it is worth your time to analyze your expenses. This is so important in our work with Profit First clients that we have a meeting dedicated to analyzing and cutting expenses.

There are two types of expenses and they are not created equal. You've probably heard the terms variable expenses and fixed expenses. Many accountants and gym mentors sometimes focus on these two elements of an expense and coach the gym owner into figuring out which expenses are variable and which are fixed.

A variable expense means the amount of the expense will likely change as revenue changes. So, if I decide to sell KT tape in my gym, I would ask, "Does the cost of KT tape increase as my revenue increases?" Well, yes it does. If I sell $100 worth of KT tape, maybe my expense is $50. If I sell $1,000 of KT tape, my expense is probably $500. As my revenue increases, so does the variable expense.

A fixed expense means the amount of the expense is the same each month regardless of the amount of revenue. Our gym currently leases its space. Does the landlord care how much my revenue is? No, because I have a contract that sets the price of the rent. It's the same every month. Whether I have $5,000 in revenue or $50,000 in revenue, rent expense is the same every month.

The best part about knowing whether your expenses are variable or fixed is nothing. That information is completely worthless. Knowledge of these two classifications does not help you make better business decisions. Rather than focus on variable or fixed, we teach that you should focus on productive expenses or nonproductive expenses. Here's why: Understanding that the amount of money I spend on KT tape increases as I sell more tells me nothing about my business decision to sell KT tape in the first place. Do my members even want to buy KT tape? Does spending money on KT tape produce value for me? It doesn't if that KT tape is just going to sit on the shelf next to my dusty supplements no one buys and next to all these T-shirts no one wants. Who cares if my rent amount stays the same every month? What's more important is if I am utilizing the space sufficiently. Could I sublease some space to offset some costs? Am I operating at maximum floor efficiency?

I sat down with Stu Brauer, creator of Microgym University and WTF Gym Talk to share with him the five questions we teach our Profit First clients about productive expenses. I find his "tell it as he sees it" approach refreshing, and his insights were a nice addition to our five questions. They are:

1. **Will this expense help generate immediate income?**
   Early on at CrossFit GSL we were looking at adding nutrition services because our gym had never offered them. We found Healthy Steps Nutrition, which provides a turnkey nutrition service. They obviously don't provide their services for free. There was a setup fee and an ongoing monthly fee. Taking on those costs could generate immediate income for us, so this a productive expense.

   Sometimes it isn't as obvious as that. Stu said, "I've seen owners tell me they are going to sell their 10 Assault Air Bikes and buy 10 new Rogue Echo Bikes. Is that price difference for a perceived nicer bike going to add income? No. Or when the owner's telling me they need more barbells. Do you? You can't be a little more creative with your workout flow? Or how about when they want to drop $5k on building signage because they think that is going to bring in new members. Save your money, get a big truck tire and put your logo on that."

2. **Does this expense serve our clients?**

   Those Atlas Stones look awesome! Our gym has some Atlas Stones that sat outside for more than twelve months, untouched. Available for anyone to steal, yet no one has stolen them. We still haven't used them in a weekday workout. Will our members find them awesome? Nope. Not a productive expense. Shiny new equipment can be tempting, but will it really provide a better service to our clients? "Gym owners are going to struggle with this question." Stu explains. "They want the new equipment. They want to use it themselves. They are going to try to connect the dots and justify how novelty equipment will serve their clients. Hopefully they have a trusted voice of reason in their lives." He also provided the example of when a client wanted to spend a lot of extra money on a reclaimed wood front desk. You've never had a cancellation because your front desk wasn't nice enough. You might get a compliment, but it isn't really serving your clients. Having a clean gym serves your clients. It doesn't generate revenue, but clean bathrooms serves an expectation our members have.

3. **Does this expense support systems that serve our clients?**

   Do you pay for programming? Programming is a system that serves your clients. That could be productive. Also, cleaning supplies support our gym cleaning system and processes. In my conversation with Stu, we came to the conclusion that this question is more valuable if the gym owner actually is aware of their systems. You have systems even if they aren't documented. Being aware of them will help you be more accurate when asking this question.

4. **Does this expense save you time?**

   This question only works if you can afford to leverage money to give yourself more time. It's okay if you are not at a point where you can do this yet. Start somewhere when you can and, slowly, you will take the low-impact tasks off your plate so you can focus on the higher-impact tasks that could really move the needle for your gym. One of the first tasks you should take off your list is cleaning the gym space. As soon as feasible, hire out that service. You may also consider how much time using a bulldog scrubber can save versus hand mopping. Leveraging your time or getting tools that allow you to do things faster frees you up to spend that time on growing the gym or improving services. Stu adds, "Spending money to save time only works if you use the time you saved."

5. **Is this expense absolutely necessary to keep the business open?**
This question is difficult to answer because microgyms could technically have classes in a park, which means no rent expense, no expense for other coaches, no utilities, no need to clean anything. That being said, in our gym's case, my partner and I both have other businesses. Neither of us have the technical ability to teach a class, so paying our coaches is absolutely necessary in order for our gym to stay open. You can continue on that line of thought and argue that to keep members happy and coming back means providing a space to work out in that has some minimal level of equipment. Maybe also a toilet… probably.

Stu says, "If gym owners are honest with themselves, the answer will likely be 'no'. It's the mindset of resources vs being resourceful. You don't need a rower for every member in the class. Choose to be resourceful and you'll figure out how to get them a good workout."

Accountants want things to fit into formulas, and these questions don't fit into a formula. Your answers will be subjective based on your goals and vision, and that is totally okay. If it is an expense you have been paying for such a long time, it can be hard for you to separate the *familiarity* of the expense from the *necessity* of the expense, so you really have to dig to get to the right answer.

Even the gyms you know and the mentors you follow have to constantly monitor spending. Knowing all these principles and having used Profit First personally and helping hundreds of gym owners do the same, I still find our gym has expenses that are not productive. I may not have them for very long thanks to the tools in this chapter, but I still have them. Whether a gym is super large or itty bitty, the goal should be to have productive expenses.

MORE KEY QUESTIONS

In addition to the five questions that help us determine the productive nature of the expense, four questions help us analyze whether or not we should cut an expense. While these four questions may appear to duplicate or overlap the five productive questions, they are in fact giving a different perspective to consider.

1. **Can you identify the actual benefit you get from spending that money?** Even better, can you come up with a dollar amount in revenue or savings generated because you spent that money?

2. **Can you get the same outcome by *not* spending money?** Really take time to see if you can come up with something. Take to Google, ask other gym owners, task your team members to answer that question.

3. **Can you get the same outcome by spending *less* money?** Sometimes an expense is unavoidable, but that doesn't mean that you couldn't find a less expensive solution.

4. **Does the expense serve your top clients or your top money-making services and programs?** As gym owners, we are not immune to shiny object syndrome. Sometimes that shiny object isn't a tangible thing, but a service we offer. This fourth question can steer us to simplify what we are

doing. We have found that sometimes when we take a step back and see the cash going into a revenue stream plus the amount of time we spend on it compared to the profit that comes out of it, the revenue stream isn't something that should be a current focus.

These nine questions are game changers to keep gym expenses as lean as possible. We encourage you to use them on every single expense that you have, whether you consider your gym already profitable or you are trying to get there.

ANALYZE EXPENSES TO CUT EXPENSES

In *Profit First*, Mike provides a ten-step process to first analyze and then cut expenses. I've included them here because the steps work. Following the steps ensures that each expense has a purpose, and that purpose is productive.

Step 1. Gather all of your bank statements and credit card statements from the last twelve months. Get them in a format that allows you to mark them up.

Step 2. Draw a box around any team member expenses. This includes payments to coaches, front desk staff, joy girls or boys; commissions; any payment to any team member. You also want to include payments you've received for coaching classes. Put a box around those numbers.

Step 3. Highlight all productive expenses. We recommend using the five productive questions to figure this out and we strongly encourage you to be brutally honest with yourself.

Step 4. Circle any repeating expenses that you plan to have in the future, whether those repeat each month, every three months, once a year. Circle those. For example, I pay a large sum for our tax software, and that is an annual expense. I would circle that one because that is absolutely necessary to keep Incite Tax open. Maybe for you it's an annual licensing fee or your annual insurance payment. At this point you may notice that some expenses have a box around them and are also highlighted and are also circled. That is just fine.

Step 5. Add up all of the expenses that you just boxed, circled, or highlighted and then divide the total by twelve. This is your average monthly expenses. Some refer to this as your monthly nut... mainly because they have a high affinity toward squirrels.

Step 6. Consider reducing or completely eliminating commissions or bonuses. I'm not saying that if you have a compensation structure for coaches that is a percentage of revenue they generate that you need to cut those coaches. Paying coaches on a percentage basis is one of many viable compensation structures. Still, if the gym is bleeding cash, and your Cash Flow Analysis shows you need to cut back on operating expenses, you may want to cut the "nice to have" bonuses or commissions... at least for now.

Step 7. Stop all automatic withdrawals from your bank account. If you highlighted the expense, you can keep those for now, but all the other auto drafts need to stop immediately.

Step 8. Call your credit card company and ask them to reissue you a new card with a new number and tell them that no charges should be accepted on the old card. Now vendors who have your card on file will have to reach out to you to get payment. When you have the conversation with the vendor, you can consider, "Do I want this expense going forward?" And it gives you the chance to negotiate better pricing or terms.

Step 9. Go through the expenses you highlighted, circled, and boxed and see if you can get rid of the expense or renegotiate it.

Step 10. Go through all the other expenses that haven't been marked and cut them. Cut all of them. If you did the previous nine steps then you know that, if the expense isn't marked, it isn't necessary for the business. If you cut too deep, guess what? You can add them back later. When it comes to making your gym healthy, stopping the bleeding, or taking your gym to the next level, these ten steps are worth your time.

TEAM MEMBER EXPENSES

Did your Cash Flow Analysis indicate your team member costs are too high? As I pointed out in Chapter 8, 44% is still respectable even though we know 25% is better. It's possible you consciously want to keep your team member costs at 44% instead of figuring out how to get it to 25%. If that fits with your vision, then don't let someone tell you otherwise.

However, if your team member costs are above 44%, then we need to at least get the percentage down to that TAP. For most microgyms, team members are your highest cost. Paying more than 44% of Real Revenue for team members means the gym is overstaffed (team members aren't producing enough revenue for what they are paid or the gym has too many classes with poor attendance), or the gym has poor compensation models, or the gym owner stepped out of the coaching role a little too soon. Or it could be any combination of those three things. If you need to get to below 44% or are trying to take your percentage down to 25%, then consider those three scenarios to see what action steps you can take to reduce your team member costs.

We've found the best place to start is to make a list of your "A" players. Sometimes we have to make judgment calls and those can be difficult because we are basically judging people and our judgment could cause them to seek employment elsewhere. Still, we all know the difference between an A player coach worth keeping and a coach not worth it. Keep the A players.

The next thing I like to do is make an organization chart, sometimes referred to as "a pain in the butt." We aren't looking for something special here. Don't buy software or spend any time on Google to find a free option to create this. Pen and paper will get the job done. We also have an example on our resource page at www.ProfitFirstForMicrogyms.com/tools.

Start your chart by noting the different positions your gym needs. You are not drawing out the positions your gym has, just what the gym needs. Do you need a general manager? A front desk attendant? A cleaner? Coaches? A head coach? Personal trainers? Group fitness trainers? Marketing manager? Sales manager? Nutrition coach? Accountant?

Next, I recommend figuring out the dollar amount you are working with. If my goal is to get to 44% of Real Revenue, I multiply my Real Revenue by 44%. If I'm trying to get to 25%, I multiply Real Revenue by 25%. Write that dollar amount on your organization chart.

Now we need to allocate that money to the different roles our gym absolutely needs. For my gym I would start with coaches. You may decide to start with a different role you feel your gym absolutely needs. Just make sure you are starting with the most absolute need first.

For my example, next to your coaches box on your organization chart, write down the amount of money needed to pay them. Now subtract the money needed to pay coaches from the total team member cost number you wrote down. If your number is now negative, then you can stop. It means you need to readjust your compensation models for coaches or look at reducing classes.

At our gym, I separate the group class coaches from the personal training and nutrition coaches because our personal trainers and nutrition coaches get a percentage of the income and not a flat fee. If there is money left over, then let's continue to the next most absolutely necessary position within the gym. Who is that for you? Is it the general manager? If so, then write down how much money you need to fairly compensate a general manager. Now subtract that money from your running balance. If the number is negative, then you can't pay a general manager that much money, unless you also adjust your coaches' compensation. Or it means that maybe there are some responsibilities you need to keep and have a general manager take over what you can afford as you keep growing the gym.

Basically, as we reduce our original dollar amount by the cost of each position, whenever the number reaches negative it means we can't afford to hire the remaining positions. As the owner, you'll probably need to step into those roles until you can afford to hire out that work. Without Profit First, you could be tempted to just reduce your take-home pay and keep these other positions. That model is not sustainable, and you will eventually burn out. If you burn out, you are no longer in a position to help change people's lives. This form of short-term sacrifice only puts long-term motivations in jeopardy.

As long as there is remaining cash, keep working down the list of absolutely necessary positions. After you have established what your gym can currently afford based on the organization chart you created, now plug in your list of A players for the roles you can afford. After those roles are assigned, you may find that some of your current team members are not on your organization chart. It's time to let them go, and that can be a difficult conversation and an emotional one. These are probably people you really enjoy working with. Your gym simply can't afford them right now.

Once you've cut the team members who needed to be cut, you should have a sit-down with your remaining team and explain to them what happened, why you made the decisions, and even walk them through how you made the decisions. This will let them know that what you just did added a level of stability to the gym, and it should make them feel good that you recognize and value what they have done for you.

We know how hard it is to survive, much less grow, in this industry. We know that people think you make more than you do. We know that there are personal relationships that make it hard to make tough business decisions. At the end of the day, you have to do what's best for you and your gym and you deserve to be in a place where your business and *you* are making money.

UNDERSTANDING DEBT

It its simplest form, debt is when one person takes money from another person and promises to pay it back. Did you know debt can be "good debt" or "bad debt"? Obviously, you want to eliminate bad debt and minimize good debt. So, how do most people classify good debt?

I asked my good friend Clay Ferrer what he thought about debt. Clay's company, Rigquipment Finance, provides financing to microgyms, so he's seen it all when it comes to debt. He explained, "I tend to characterize debt as being good or bad based on what it is used for. Good debt is used to generate cash inflows over an extended period of time. Borrowing money to cover expenses is bad."

If what you bought with a debt increases your net worth or has future value, then most would consider that good debt. Common examples are your mortgage for your house, school loans (reasonable though), real estate loans, and business loans. Bad debt, on the other hand, is when you use borrowed money to buy something that immediately goes down in value. Common examples are credit card debt, auto loans, or any other type of consumer debt. Clay added, "When borrowing money for expenses, the owner will actually face an increased expense burden in the future, as they now have to pay those same expenses plus the additional cost of the debt service, and all without the benefit of any additional revenue."

Now, I'm not talking about someone trying to earn points or cashback rewards when the person pays off the credit card each month. I know of no millionaire who has said, "If it weren't for my rewards points, I would never have become a millionaire." But feel free to enjoy your points as long as you are not racking up more credit card debt.

Any of the expenses that are in the "good debt" category could just as easily be considered bad debt. You could buy a house well beyond your ability to pay for it. On the school loan, investing in your education is awesome, and that is why people consider this good debt. Could you have got the same education for a cheaper tuition fee? Or did you flip flop on majors so many times that you were in school for years longer than you needed to be? You can always make a bad real estate deal and if you don't know anything about the business you are investing in or buying, that could be really bad debt too.

Only you can decide if you've incurred good debt or bad debt. If you aren't sure, the answer is always, don't go into debt, don't borrow that money until you are sure it's a good decision. I have seen lots of clients lose their shirts (metaphorically speaking of course) because they were so dumb about their debt load.

GETTING OUT OF DEBT

A very common approach to paying down debt, and one which we recommend, is called the debt snowball. Everybody we know gives credit to Dave Ramsey for coming up with this, so we will too.

The first step is to list your debts in order, from lowest to highest balances owed. Do not organize your debt based on interest rates. While it's true mathematically that, if you pay off the highest interest rates first, you would pay less interest over time, most people who try to pay off highest interest rates first end up never getting out of debt. We need small victories to keep feeling motivated. That's why we like this method.

Let's use an example so you can see how the debt snowball works. This is super simple, and the concept is easy to grasp. Here is a list of debts with the loan balance and the minimum payment. I think it's important to note I'm not wasting energy on unnecessary details such as interest rate or date the loan is due. The reason is that, on the majority of loans, as long as you make the minimum payment you are never past due.

	Total owed	Minimum Payment
Car loan	$23,450	$345
Past due vendor invoices	$1,815	$0
Mortgage	$399,000	$2,800
Personal loan from family members	$50,000	$200
Business loan	$140,000	$1,200

Now, it's important to note that your mortgage is not usually listed in a debt snowball strategy. Lots of people think about paying off their house as a larger long-term financial goal. I will continue to make my monthly mortgage payments, but I won't include that in my debt snowball list. Here is how I would order those debts for my debt snowball list (lowest balance to highest balance).

	Total owed	Minimum Payment
Past due vendor invoices	$1,815	$0
Car loan	$23,450	$345
Personal loan from family members	$50,000	$200
Business loan	$140,000	$1,200

In this example, the total minimum payment amount each month is $1,745. Now that I've gone through my expenses and have found some extra cash flow, I can see that I have an extra $250 per month that I can use to help me get out of debt. Starting with my lowest-balance debt of $1,815, I will make the minimum payment of $0 plus the $250. It would take me seven months to pay off the past due vendor invoices. Once they are paid off, I now move to the next debt. (This also assumes that by using Profit First you are committing to not taking on any new debt. If you did, you need to update your debt list.)

The car loan would be the next one on the list. Since I've been making my minimum monthly payments, after seven months the balance would be $22,000. I pay the minimum of $345 plus the $250

I was using for the previous debt. Once that debt is paid off, I then move to the $50,000 personal loan. I pay its minimum $200 payment plus the $345 plus the $250. Do you see how the payment amounts increase as each debt gets paid off, just as a snowball grows larger and larger as it rolls down the hill?

PROFIT DISTRIBUTION TIME

In the previous example, I used normal operating expense money to work the debt snowball. In order to get out of debt faster, you *have* to pay more toward the principals than the minimum payment amount. It's the only way. The same is especially true if your minimum payment is only covering the interest amount.

How does Profit First help you pay down debt faster? For starters, you clean up your operating expenses so that you now have more funds available to work the debt snowball in the normal course of business. But wait, there's more!

When you get to quarterly profit distribution time, you can use your profit distribution to pay off additional debt principal. This is one of the benefits of living your life within the OWNER'S PAY amount and not relying on profit distributions for your lifestyle. The quarterly profit distribution is just gravy, as they say, whoever "they" are.

So, if I had a quarterly profit distribution of $5,000 and I was still working on my car loan with my debt snowball payment of $595, by paying the profit distribution of $5,000 toward my loan balance, I just shortened how long it will take me to pay off that loan by almost a year. That is how you destroy debt.

We have an Excel file available for download that makes it easy to list your debts and see what it looks like to work your debt snowball at www.ProfitFirstForMicrogyms.com/tools.

TRIDENT CROSSFIT

In *Profit First*, Mike shared a story of a friend who found himself in a situation where the bank was demanding he pay off his million-dollar loan. Then Mike shared how he encouraged his friend to focus on profits and the Profit First system. Mike said, "Why was I talking about profit when he was so far in the hole? You may be feeling this way, too. I get it. It's awfully hard to think about profit, let alone plan for it, when your situation is …dire."

Going into 2018, Trident CrossFit was carrying over $60,000 of credit card debt that had basically been there since 2016. For more than two years, they were hit with a never-ending barrage of interest charges—a pound of flesh of $1,000 a month, roughly. The owner, Chriss Smith explained that, despite many attempts, they could not seem to find a way to make a dent in the principal balance.

Eryn Smith, a former CrossFit affiliate owner and one of our firm's Profit First ninjas, made it her sole mission to eradicate that credit card debt. Can you imagine what you could do with an extra $1,000 per month? That money at the time was just getting flushed down the toilet.

Trident CrossFit has really strong revenue. Their monthly income puts them in the top echelon of microgyms when it comes to top line revenue. Unfortunately, they were spending all of it. They had the mindset that the more they make, the better things will be. With that focus, the top line did increase, but you have to figure out how to keep it too. Mike said, "Well-dressed poverty is still poverty. Just because your business is making lots of money doesn't mean you're hanging on to it." In their case, they were spending all of it.

With Eryn as their Profit First coach, Trident CrossFit came up with a plan using concepts from this chapter to cut unnecessary expenses. They committed to stop using the credit cards and forced the business to cover expenses so they could get to work on cutting down this debt. They even created a plan to reduce their OWNER'S PAY amounts for the short term (while still covering their personal bills) to free up additional cash to eliminate the $60,000. They were laser-focused on destroying the debt. In addition, they elected to do weekly allocation days instead of using the 10/25 rhythm. They also used their profit distributions and applied those to the debt balance.

With all of these efforts in place, they were able to completely eliminate $60,000 worth of debt in just five months. Not only were they saving $1,000 in interest expense, but they were able to free up the cash flow they had been using to pay down the credit card balances. In total, it was closer to $8,000 of freed up cash flow each month they could now play with. Eight thousand that wasn't needed for the daily operations. Eight thousand they could choose to use to increase their profit distribution, OWNER'S PAY or even tinker with the gym. What they couldn't do in more than two years on their own, they were able to accomplish in five months with the Profit First system and the tools and resources that are in this book.

FINANCIAL WORKOUT

Next time you are going to take on a new expense or next time you sit down to look at your cash flow, ask the five productive questions and the four more questions about each expense. This should happen within the next fifteen days.

Also, go through the ten steps of analyzing your expenses. Think of it as a treasure hunt. Get excited about it. Cutting expenses is like finding treasure that you can use to make your gym that much healthier. The ten steps might be a task you aren't sure you can do. That's why we broke it up into ten steps. Take it one step at a time and you'll be amazed at how quickly you can analyze your expenses.

CHAPTER 10

GYM TAX STRATEGIES TO INCREASE CASH FLOW

A S I SAID EARLIER, CASH FLOW IS THE LIFEBLOOD OF ANY GYM. Cut off the cash flow, and the gym will die. Profit First ensures cash flows in and out of your gym in a healthy, sustainable way. One of those cash outflows is income taxes. In fact, income taxes will be one of your largest lifetime expenses. In this chapter, we focus on your TAX account. Specifically, you'll learn strategies you can use so you won't need as much cash for your taxes.

You've already learned that the tax burden should be covered by the gym's revenue and you've learned how to allocate Real Revenue to this smaller plate. You've also learned when to do it and how much Real Revenue to transfer to your TAX account.

Now we will talk about the different ways you can reduce the tax burden. The lower you can keep the percentage you allocate to taxes, the higher you can keep your OWNER'S PAY, PROFIT, and/or OPEX. I have to add, though, as always, I'm giving you my best here, but you should always consult with a professional regarding your specific situation. (I happen to know a great firm you could use. Wink. Wink.)

At our gym, which is probably similar to yours, we like to see what our new members are capable of when they start. We use an assessment to do this. In the tax world, we do the same thing with our clients. We need to assess their starting point, and that begins with the entity they chose for their gym.

The word entity means "something that exists in itself, a thing with distinct and independent existence."[1] In simple terms, it is referring to the legal structure for your gym. I'm just going to cover some of the

---

[1] Memidex 2019, http://www.memidex.com/entity, accessed November 24, 2019

more common entity options instead of every single option. Because the entity you choose also has legal implications and consequences, you also want to talk this over with an attorney familiar with your state laws.

Here are the entities we will review in this chapter:

- Sole Proprietor
- Single-member LLC
- Multi-member LLC
- S Corporation
- C Corporation

SOLE PROPRIETOR

From a tax standpoint, this is the worst possible tax scenario because of the way the IRS classifies income earned from a gym. The IRS calls it "ordinary" income. Ordinary income has the opportunity (as the IRS refers to it) to pay self-employment tax on the taxable income. This curse (as everyone else sees it) is a 15.3% tax as of 2020. Well, that tax rate doesn't seem bad. Hold on! The 15.3% self-employment tax is on top of the income tax rate you are already paying. So even if a gym had $20,000 of taxable income, the owner could be paying 40% total tax on that. This high combined tax rate is why this tax structure is the least useful for your gym, especially since there are better options available to you.

Another reason being a sole proprietor sucks is that you file all your gym activity on Schedule C of your personal tax return. Who cares, right? You care. Here's why: Personal returns with a Schedule C have an extremely high rate of having an IRS audit, more than double the chance of other forms. Don't believe us? Feel free to google "what percentage of Schedule C are audited?" Spoiler alert: Any number of the search results will confirm our statement.

SINGLE MEMBER LLC

From a legal standpoint, a single-member LLC (an LLC that has one owner) is a step up from being a sole proprietor, but that is where the benefit ends. From a tax standpoint, a single-member LLC is taxed *exactly* like a sole proprietor. The IRS doesn't even call them single-member LLCs, for crying out loud. They call them "disregarded" entities, meaning they give them no regard. They don't exist to the IRS. This means the default treatment for a single-member LLC is to file on Schedule C (I just explained why that's bad), and the taxable income gets the fun additional 15.3% self-employment tax on top of the income tax rate. Same terrible tax rate and same terrible audit risk.

That being said, you can make an election to tax your single-member LLC as an S corporation or a C Corporation, which makes it something completely different for tax purposes. I'll say more on that in the S Corporation and C Corporation sections. Also note that I'm providing general guidelines and principles. A single-member LLC when effectively used for specific tax strategies is amazing. However, for your microgym income, it's not an ideal structure.

MULTI-MEMBER LLC

Here's the deal with LLCs. They were created in 1977 in Wyoming, and nearly fifty years isn't enough time for the IRS to understand them. So, they basically force all LLCs, whether they have one member or more than one member, to be taxed like something else that already exists in the tax code.

A multi-member LLC is an LLC that has more than one member. Hence the "multi" part. The IRS taxes a multi-member LLC like a partnership. That means, for an active member, such as a gym owner who is teaching classes or doing anything involved in the day-to-day operations, they also get to pay that ridiculous 15.3% self-employment tax, just like a sole proprietor, just like a single-member LLC. If you are not involved in the day-to-day, you are considered a passive owner and you would not have to worry about that 15.3% self-employment tax.

The biggest difference between a multi-member LLC and a single member LLC is that a multi-member LLC has its own tax return. This means the chance of being audited by the IRS is less for a multi-member LLC than a single-member LLC or a sole proprietor. What happens then is that this separate partnership tax return creates a K-1 statement for each member (which is another way to say owner). Just as an employee gets a W-2 and an independent contractor gets a 1099, a member of a multi-member LLC gets a K-1. This ensures that the business itself isn't paying income tax. Instead, each owner files the K-1 income statement with their personal return where the tax owed on that income is calculated.

S CORPORATION

The S Corporation is similar to a multi-member LLC in that it has its own separate tax filing and it creates a K-1 for the shareholders (owners). So just like on the multi-member LLC, the S Corporation does not pay a separate income tax. The taxable income is reported on the K-1, and the owners use that info on their personal return to figure out how much they owe in taxes.

The S Corporation is different in two big ways, though. The first is that the taxable income of the business does not incur the 15.3% self-employment tax. You do not pay that on the taxable income of an S Corporation. The second is that, because the IRS doesn't get to steal that 15.3% from you, it requires any shareholder who works in the business to issue themselves a W-2. The tax code refers to this as a "reasonable wage."

This is the most complicated aspect of the S Corporation and usually involves a conversation with our clients so they can understand what these requirements mean for them. So please hang with me and don't let your eyes glaze over from the boring, yet complicated, tax talk. The punchline to this section is that almost all microgym owners need an S Corporation in their tax structure. And for many, all they need is the S Corporation in order to maximize tax savings.

So let me first address whether you need to worry about this idea of a "reasonable wage." If you are involved in the day-to-day activities of your gym, then you are a shareholder-employee.

If you work in any capacity in the gym, even if sporadically, the IRS expects to see you pay yourself a "reasonable wage" for that work, so you would still be a shareholder-employee. Maybe you are thinking that you can avoid this if you have your spouse become the owner of the microgym so that you can avoid this classification of shareholder-employee. Unfortunately, the IRS gets you there, too. If you are the only one working in the gym, then you would be considered an "officer," and the tax code still makes you pay yourself a "reasonable wage." If the only other team members you have are coaches who only coach classes, you are still going to be considered an officer as well.

What is a reasonable wage? Unfortunately, or luckily (depends whether you are a glass half full or glass half empty person), the IRS does not define for us what *reasonable* means. There is no magic formula. It's always a "facts and circumstances" test. The tax courts over the years have issued lots of decisions relating to this, so most guidelines come from court cases. I can tell you from the court cases we have read, most people get themselves in trouble when they don't claim any wages—meaning zero wages paid to themselves. They want to classify everything as a distribution, because if everything is a distribution, then they pay zero self-employment tax.

We want you to minimize as much of this self-employment tax as possible. But zero is not likely. We can, however, keep your "reasonable wage" as low as possible. You will receive this "reasonable wage" in the form of a W-2 because you are an employee of your own business. Issuing yourself a W-2 means that you pay payroll tax on those wages. As the employer and the employee, it's the same 15.3% we've discussed earlier. Since a zero wage isn't an option, we want to pay the smallest wage amount possible to still be considered reasonable. Again, there is no magic formula to determine "reasonable." I can't tell you the exact amount you should pay yourself in the form of a W-2. The best I can do is give you the guidelines the tax courts use. (Please note I'm translating this into human. If you really want to geek out about it check out the footnote.[2])

---

[2] IRS, "Reasonable Compensation: Job Aid for IRS Valuation Professional," Octo-

1. Your skillset and experience
2. The actual work you are doing for your gym and the amount of time you spend doing it
3. Your Total Revenue and level of complexity in your service offerings
4. Your W-2 amount as a percentage of Total Revenue and Net Income
5. The overall health of the fitness industry and economy
6. Your wages compared to amounts paid to other owners
7. Market rate for people with similar titles in the fitness industry
8. The wage policy of the business for all employees
9. Your W-2 amounts in past years

The end result should always be that the wage amount is less than the net income of the gym. This means that, unlike the other entity scenarios described, we know with an S Corporation that 100% of the net income is not going to be hit with the 15.3% self-employment tax. To illustrate, let's consider a gym that has $50,000 in net income. After the guidelines are reviewed, a $20,000 wage is recommended as reasonable. You would pay $4,590 less in self-employment tax compared to what a sole proprietor (or a single member LLC taxed as a sole proprietor or as an active partner in a multi-member LLC) would pay. I have always thought the tax savings is worth the slightly more complicated tax structure. It's only more complicated because you have to do payroll filings to record your W-2 earnings.

At this point in the conversation, you might interject with this statement, "But I can't live on $20,000. I need more than that." That's not a problem. We are not suggesting you only live on the $20,000. The $20,000 W-2 is just to stay compliant with the tax code. Your take-home pay is still going to be the OWNER'S PAY amount from your Cash Flow Analysis. So in this example, the Profit First OWNER'S PAY amount is $42,000. Since $20,000 is being reported as W-2 income, then the other $22,000 will be a distribution.

Don't let the tax side conflict with the Profit First side. I actually debated whether to include this chapter because I didn't want to confuse any component of the Profit First system. Ultimately, I felt the cash savings from paying less in taxes is so important that I needed to keep this chapter in here for you. Just remember, Profit First plays very nicely and works great with tax savings strategies. The tax savings strategies will never affect the way you run Profit First for your microgym.

C CORPORATION

The last entity to cover ever so briefly is a C Corporation. Unlike the other entities discussed, a C Corporation pays taxes at the corporate level. Shareholders do not receive a K-1 from the C Corporation. If they take a distribution, the tax code calls that a dividend, and if they do get a dividend, they claim that dividend as taxable income on their personal tax return. Here is where C Corporations suck. Those dividends were already taxed at the corporate level first. Then the owner pays taxes on the personal level. This is known as "double taxation" and is the most common reason referenced as to why you probably don't want a C corporation. In the gym industry, the C Corporation is rarely a good choice.

For good measure, here's a basic example of double taxation. Let's say the C Corporation has $50,000 in net income. The 2019 Corporate tax rate is 21%. So the gym would owe $10,500 in income tax. Let's say the gym pays the rest of the cash to you. We started with $50,000, paid $10,500 in taxes, so the other $39,500 is paid to you in the form of a dividend. Even assuming they qualify for the better capital gains rate, which they likely will not, you will pay 15% on that and, let's assume, another 5% for state tax, which is another $7,900. That means you actually get to use $31,600. Or said in another way, you would have paid $18,400 in taxes which is a 37% tax rate. That's brutal!

WHAT CAN I WRITE OFF?

"Can I write this off on my taxes?" is one of the most common questions we receive at Incite Tax. The way the tax code answers that question is by saying your business expense needs to be both "ordinary" and "necessary." Oh, great! That is a super helpful definition. (Not!) So the IRS had to answer their first answer with a definition of their first definition. (That is, by the way, the main reason the tax code is 75,000-plus pages long.)

IRS defines an "ordinary expense" as one that is common and accepted in your trade and business. A "necessary expense" is one that is helpful and appropriate for your trade and business. The definition should be clearer because they are using more words, but the true meaning seems hard to grasp. The easiest way to break that down is this: Is this expense somehow related to my business?

If there is business purpose to the expense, which means it would fall under the IRS distinction of ordinary and necessary, then you would claim it as a business deduction and pay for it out of your Profit First OPEX account.

One of the best habits you can create is to always ask yourself, "Is this expense somehow related to my business?" That should help you figure out what you can claim on your taxes. I now want to cover a few really common deductions that should be on your mind.

HOW DO I WRITE OFF TRAVEL EXPENSES?

Who doesn't like to get away every once in a while? Actually, I don't. I love the great indoors and I love stay-cations. My house has almost everything I want, including a gigantic TV, super comfortable couch, and my amazeballs mattress. I get that I'm a weirdo, and most people enjoy taking vacations. So, how do you turn travel into a business expense?

Let's keep the question train rolling. Where can you find customers? Where can you research things that can improve your business? Where might you consider opening a new location?

Where can you find other microgym owners to collaborate in their space and get tours of their facilities and see how they operate?

For gym owners, the answer is, "almost anywhere." So with a little bit of planning, you could deduct your trips anywhere in the world if you can connect the travel with your gym. What exactly can you write off with business travel? Your cost to get there and return home, your lodging costs, and your food costs while on the trip.

What does the IRS say about this? The overall concept is that, if more than half of your travel days are considered for business purposes, then you can deduct the trip. The day you are actually traveling is considered a business day. This means you have at least two business days already since you need to travel to and return from the destination. Basically, add up the number of days of the trip, divide by two, and make sure at least that many days have a business purpose. Also, if you are traveling over a weekend and Friday and Monday have business purposes, Saturday and Sunday are automatically defined as having business purpose.

The IRS says a travel day is any day you are sleeping away from your home for a business reason. If you stayed at a hotel that is next door to your home, that could still be considered a travel day.

The IRS says a business day is when you conduct business or meet with someone for a "bona fide" business reason regardless of how long the business stuff is happening. So maybe you visit another microgym and go to their five a.m. class. That whole day is a business day, even if you spent the rest of it at Disneyland.

The really important thing about travel days if you are audited by the IRS is that you have to show that you preplanned the business purpose of your travel. You can't fly to Cancun and hope you have a business conversation so that you can count it as a write-off. You have to prove to the IRS the reason you went to Cancun was for business and then, if it so happens you have personal fun while there, they can't do anything about it.

HOW DO I WRITE OFF MY CAR OR TRUCK?

One of the most often asked questions that we get from our clients, and really anyone once they find out we do taxes, is how can they write off their car. Have you wondered if you should title the car in your business name? Do you need to wrap your vehicle in your company logo to be able to take a tax deduction? Do you have to

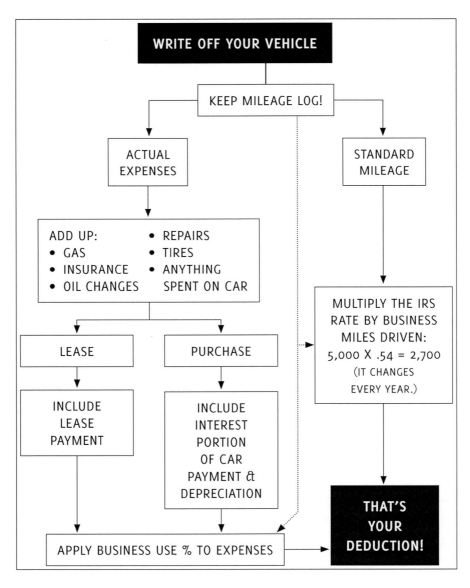

buy a monster truck for the tax deduction to work? The tax rules for automobile expenses are not straightforward. Let's start at the five-thousand-foot view and get an understanding of the basic rules and then we will dig into the other aspects of the rules that aren't as straightforward.

On the top of the decision tree you have two options on how to write off your vehicle. You cannot choose both; you have to pick one. Option 1 is you can deduct what you actually spend on the vehicle, or Option 2 you can take a standard mileage deduction based on the business miles you're claiming. Those are the two options. One or the other. Not both. If audited, you would need to be able to show a mileage log no matter which option you choose.

OPTION 1: ACTUAL EXPENSES
The following expenses are all considered actual expenses:

- gas you put into the car
- insurance
- oil changes
- any other types of repairs
- changing brake pads
- windshields
- tires
- anything that is spent on your car

Why isn't the monthly car payment in that list? Because the actual expense is different depending on whether you are leasing it or purchasing it. That's why this is the next part of the decision tree.

If you are leasing the vehicle, your lease payment is just a fancy way to say you are renting. Because it's rent, your entire lease payment is claimed as an actual expense.

If you are purchasing the vehicle, your entire payment is not an actual expense. Only the interest portion of your payment is considered an actual expense. The principal portion is not. The reason is, when you receive the auto loan, the IRS doesn't make you claim that as income. So when you pay back the loan, they don't let you take it as an expense either. That being said, if you are purchasing your vehicle, you get another tax deduction for depreciation. I'm not going to go into the intricacies of how depreciation works. Basically, it's a way you can expense part of the purchase price of your vehicle, but you don't get it all in one year. The IRS makes you spread it out over a few years.

OPTION 2: STANDARD MILEAGE

This option is a lot more straightforward. You take the miles that you're claiming for business purposes and multiply by the standard IRS mileage rate. The IRS changes this rate every year, so look up what that rate is, or your tax professional will know what it is. Just make sure to give that tax professional your business mileage if they don't ask for it.

We review lots of tax returns from prospects and we often find that a lot of tax preparers are not asking gym owners for their mileage. At a minimum make sure that you give them your mileage.

The only miles you can claim, though, are the ones that are for business purposes. This doesn't mean just miles driven to the gym. It can be miles driving to get office supplies, miles to a convention you attended for business purposes. miles to the restaurant for a business meal. If you drive a mile that has any business purpose tied to it, you claim it.

After reviewing these two options with a client, typically they will interject, "I don't really want to track my miles. It seems like a lot of work. So, I'm going to just take actual expenses." Of course the IRS would never let it be that simple. Let's say after you add up all your actual expenses (gas, interest payments, oil changes, repairs, tires, etc.) you have $5,000 of auto expenses. It would be natural for you to think that you could claim that full $5,000 of actual expenses as a tax deduction. Nope. The IRS lets you take the "business use percentage" of your actual expenses.

What is your business use percentage, and more importantly, how do you figure it out? The definition is very simple. It's the percentage of your business miles compared to your total mileage, and the only way to figure it out is to divide your business miles by your total miles. The IRS assumes you use your vehicle for personal purposes unless you can prove otherwise. The only way to prove otherwise is to track your miles. It has to be done.

Back to our example. Let's say you drove 8,000 miles that year for business and 10,000 total miles. That is 80% business use percentage. You then take 80% of the $5,000, which is $4,000, and that is your tax deduction. OR... since you drove 8,000 miles you could take the standard mileage deduction. To do that you multiply your 8,000 miles by the IRS mileage rate. That mileage rate changes every year. In 2019, it is .58 cents per mile. That means your 8,000 miles is a $4,640 tax deduction. The bottom line is, whichever method you want to use, you have to track your business miles.

BONUS QUESTION #1: VEHICLE TITLE
Should you title your vehicle in your business name or personal name? It doesn't matter from a tax perspective. You can claim a tax deduction based on your mileage log whether the title is in your name or your business name. However, you should be aware that if you title your vehicle in your business name, you will need to get a business insurance policy on the vehicle that is different from the normal property and casualty insurance. Unless you have a fleet of business vehicles, we normally don't recommend titling your vehicle in the business name.

BONUS QUESTION #2: WRAP MY VEHICLE WITH A LOGO
Should you wrap your vehicle or put your business logo on your vehicle? I don't know... should you? Only wrap your vehicle if you believe it's going to benefit your business. Don't do it for the sake of the tax write-off because it's not a requirement. Nothing in the tax code says the vehicle has to have your logo on it in order to write off the miles. Your miles just have to have business purpose in order to be a tax write-off. It's that simple.

HOW DO I WRITE OFF EQUIPMENT EXPENSES?

As a microgym owner you have equipment, so it's worth mentioning just a few things about it. Tax rules tell you that when you buy some equipment you can either expense it as a repair cost, expense it as a small equipment cost, or call it an "asset." An "asset" classification means that what you bought is expected to last more than a few years. That's why the IRS says normally that means you can't take a tax deduction for the full cost of that asset. Instead they say, if it's going to last a long time, then you should only be able to take a percentage of your cost each year. The tax code refers to that as "depreciation."

Most gym equipment falls into the "asset" category. For 2019, as has been the case for many years, there always seems to be some sort of "bonus depreciation" option. This is a tax way of saying, "take the full cost as a tax deduction" on your tax return.

If I take a loan out to finance the equipment, I can still expense the full cost of the equipment. Even though I'm not using any cash to buy the equipment, I could still save real cash by paying less taxes. Of course, review Chapter 9 on debt to make sure you are taking on good debt.

HOW DO I CLASSIFY MY COACH?

In the microgym world, there are two camps of thought on paying a 1099 or a W-2 to team members. They either are *always* independent contractors or they are *always* employees. Guess what? Neither camps are correct.

I'm trying to get people into my camp, which asserts that team members could be in either classification based on how you set up the relationship. The word *always* has no place in this decision.

That is, coaches are *always* employees. Wrong. Or coaches are *always* independent contractors. Wrong. We have been in the battlefield on this, and I'm telling you without a shadow of doubt, my camp is the only one to be in.

In late 2018, we got involved in an audit being performed by Minnesota when it was looking at a CrossFit affiliate. We provided our guidance to the CrossFit affiliate on how to handle that audit along with what they need to prove their coaches were contractors, and they won. The state of Minnesota agreed the coaches were contractors.

Early 2018, we helped another microgym owner in Alaska with the same issue and we got the same result. Don't buy into the myth that coaches can't be contractors. They can, but it depends on how things are set up.

That being said, in 2018, the California Supreme Court in Dynamex Operations West v Superior Court of Los Angeles made a change in their law to the definition of an independent contractor. The big change is that a worker can't be an independent contractor if what they do is the usual part of the business. Since a microgym's primary offering is some form of training, the coaches can't be contractors in California, as of 2018. That being said, if you have other offerings, such as nutrition coaching, you should be able to show that the nutrition income isn't a usual part of your gym business and the nutrition coaches could be contractors.

It's really important you check with your state laws and not just the IRS rules I'm covering here. It's possible to have a coach who could be a contractor based on IRS rules and not be a contractor based on the state rules. In addition, you also want to check with your state's unemployment department. You can have an independent contractor, but still need to pay unemployment compensation for them even though they would get a 1099. I know; leave it to government to keep things clear as mud.

WHY DOES ALL THIS MATTER?

Too often this topic focuses on the greed of the gym owner because it is assumed the only reason for independent contractor status is so the gym owner can get out of paying the payroll tax on their payments to the contractor. People believe the contractor will have to pay that 15.3% self-employment tax we have been talking about, and that simply isn't true, especially now after the 2018 tax reform. Being an independent contractor allows one to take advantage of the tax code claiming their own business deductions using the same strategies a gym owner can use and thereby decreasing how much income they have to pay tax on. Employees pay tax on the full amount of what they received. Period. Even if they had expenses of their own. We have done the math to see, from a tax savings point of view, whether independent contractor or employee is the better status for the team member, and being an independent contractor wins about 90 percent of the time. However, you can't classify someone as a contractor just because of tax savings. In order to classify as a contractor, the relationship between you and the team member needs to fit the criteria established by the IRS and the state you live in.

(Why am I just focusing on talking to you about a contractor? The IRS has never audited a gym to look at team members that are classified as employees because they want you to keep paying the payroll tax even if you aren't legally required to pay it.)

STRAIGHTFORWARD TEST—IRS STYLE

Of course the IRS wants to help you make the right decision, so they have a test you can use to determine if your worker is an employee or an independent contractor. This test is technically called the "right to control test" because each factor is designed to evaluate who controls how the work is performed. Under IRS rules, independent contractors by definition control the manner and means by which they perform the contract and services. The more control your company exercises over how, when, where, and by whom work is performed, the more likely it is your workers are employees.

Even though the IRS thought that explanation was simple, lots of business owners struggled with understanding it. (And by "lots" I mean all.) The fact the tax code doesn't define "employee" doesn't help either. So, the IRS came out with some additional guidelines to make it clearer—twenty-four additional guidelines, to be precise.

These twenty-four factors are not created equal. Some are more important than others. Further, just because one factor may indicate an employee relationship doesn't make that worker an employee. All factors have to be considered to make a decision. This means there is no single factor that will determine the outcome. It's important to note this because IRS auditors can be (and most of the time are) big bullies. They tend to only focus on the factors that support employee status and tend to ignore the factors that support contractor status.

The IRS manual used to train the "worker classification auditors" says the three most important factors are the following:

Instructions to workers: Employees follow instructions on when, where, and how work is to be done. Independent contractors have much more flexibility in performing work as they want. But you can still dictate what you want the end result to be. Don't confuse this with hiring someone who has a specific skill set. If I have a CrossFit gym, the coaches I hire need to have at least their level 1 certification from CrossFit. That doesn't automatically make them employees.

Job Training: If your company provides, or even arranges, training of *any* kind for the worker, the IRS views this as a sign that you expect the work to be performed in a certain way; therefore, the worker is an employee. It can be as informal as requiring the worker to attend meetings or work alongside someone more experienced. This isn't to say that an independent contractor doesn't get training. It's just that the independent contractor would have to choose what training and when to get it. The independent contractor would also pay for the training.

Worker's ability to make a profit or suffer a loss: Employees can be rewarded, disciplined, demoted, even fired, based on job performance, but they always get paid. Independent contractors have to have a financial stake in their enterprise. So if an independent contractor is disciplined or fired, he would probably not get paid, or might have the projects they are performing for you reduced (like cutting back the number of classes a coach would be teaching), or at least have to discount the originally agreed-upon amount.

The IRS also puts high priority on the following ten factors:

W-2 or 1099: Employees get W-2s and contractors get 1099s.

Intent of Relationship: The worker should sign a written agreement that explains all the factors that make him a contractor.

Pay Basis: Employees are paid based on their time. Hourly, weekly, monthly, etc. Independent contractors are paid by job, project, assignment, or receive a commission which is usually a percentage of a sale.

Benefits: If you provide benefits, they are probably an employee. Independent contractors are responsible for their own benefits.

Incorporated Status: Independent contractors should consider incorporating (setting up one of those entities you learned about earlier in the chapter). It's a strong indicator that the worker is independent.

Importance of the worker's services: If a worker provides services that are integral to the success of your business, the worker is likely your employee. So, if I had a business in which I'm paying trainers to provide a bulk of the actual service, the argument I would use to claim the worker is a contractor is that my business is marketing. If the independent contractor ends up sucking, I can easily replace the contractor without affecting my business. However, I can't very easily add different marketing methods. So my marketing methods would have a much higher importance than the contractor's service.

Personal performance of services: An independent contractor should have the freedom to hire assistants or subcontract work to other workers or firms at his or her expense. If you require the worker to perform the work personally, that's a sign of control and therefore indicative of employee status.

Providing assistants: There's likely an employer-employee relationship if your company hires, supervises, and pays assistants for the worker. An independent contractor would pay for an assistant out of her own pocket.

Ongoing relationship: The worker doesn't have to work for you continuously to be considered an employee; it may be enough if the worker gets assignments at frequently recurring, even if irregular, intervals. On the flip side, an independent contractor agreement can indicate an ongoing relationship for multiple or sequential projects.

Setting the order or the sequence of the work: If you determine what gets done when, it indicates you control how the work is performed.

Allow an independent contractor to decide his or her schedule, both day-to-day and for the longer term.

The rest of the eleven factors are important but are considered less important than the ones listed.

Flexibility of schedule: If the company dictates when the worker has to show up and for how long, chances are it is an employment relationship. Independent contractors set their own schedule and can work as long as or as little as they want as long as the project or service contracted is performed.

Demands for fulltime work: Fulltime work gives a company control over most of the person's time, which would make that an employment relationship. An independent contractor probably isn't dedicating thirty hours a week to one business.

Need for onsite services: Requiring someone to work on company premises if the work can be performed elsewhere indicates an employment relationship.

Requirements for reports: Employees tend to regularly produce written or oral reports on the status of projects. Independent contractors would not be subject to something such as this and are more likely to be evaluated based on the end result.

Payment of business for travel expenses: Independent contractors pay these types of expenses. Most contractors would set their fees high enough to cover such costs. Employees get these types of expenses reimbursed.

Provisional tools and materials: Employees typically have provided to them equipment, tools, and materials. Independent contractors typically provide their own supplies or tools to support their work.

Investment in facilities: Independent contractors typically have their own workspace, while employees rely on the employer to provide the workspace.

Work for multiple companies: Workers who simultaneously provide services for other companies or people are likely to be independent contractors.

Availability to public: If the worker makes services available to the general public, they're probably an independent contractor.

Control over discharge: A company unilaterally has the right to discharge a worker such as an employee. The other side of the token, the company's ability to terminate independent contractors generally depends on contract terms.

Right of termination: Most employees can terminate their work with the company without liability. Independent contractors cannot terminate services voluntarily, except as their contract allows.

NEVER ALWAYS

Needless to say, these tests are a perfect example of how crazy and "not-simple" making a decision can be. It is also why the two camps of always an employee or always an independent contractor don't make sense with the 1099 versus W-2 issue. It also means, if you want the team member to be a contractor, you have to structure the relationship within these twenty-four points so they qualify. As you can see, that means you give up some control in certain areas. Maybe you like the idea of saving on payroll taxes while helping your team members have a better tax outcome as independent contractors, and maybe you like the simplicity of just making everyone an employee. Neither answer is wrong.

FINANCIAL WORKOUT

I totally accept that you probably don't find taxes as sexy as I do. Maybe though, what you find very sexy, is all the things you can buy because you aren't overpaying your taxes. This chapter offers a lot of different areas for you to consider. Do you have the right entity to maximize tax savings? Are you taking advantage of all the deductions the tax code offers? Are you classifying your team members properly?

CHAPTER 11

TRACKING KEY PREDICTIVE INDICATORS

I MAGINE HAVING SIX DIFFERENT GYM LOCATIONS, AND SOME ARE in different states. How many hours would you imagine you have to spend keeping those locations running? If I take the headaches I have now with just one location, would I multiply that by six? Or would having five more locations be exponentially more difficult than just one? What if I told you six locations spread out over different states has been done before, and the owner only worked five hours per week? That's not five hours per location. That's five hours *period*.

I first learned about Lisa Kuecker when I read Mike's book, *Clockwork*. Lisa not only took a failing studio and turned it into a seven-figure business, but also at her peak ran five additional microgym and boutique studio locations that ended with a seven-figure sales price. She has since launched a thriving consulting business helping other microgym and studio owners do the same. The part of her story that made her so memorable for me was that, when she was running those six locations, she averaged five hours of work per week.

What role did Key Predictive Indicators (KPIs) have in keeping her hours down? Lisa says, "Everything."

A KPI is a number that is important or in other words, a number that is "key" to your gym that also tells you something about how your gym is performing.

There are two types of KPIs: a lagging indicator or a leading indicator. A lagging indicator gives you information about something that has happened in the past. A leading indicator can tell you about what is going to happen; it basically allows you to predict the outcome before it happens.

While it is good to have metrics that will shed light on how the gym is performing, whenever possible, if you can find a number that predicts how the gym *will be* performing, that is always best. That's why we call them Key Predictive Indicators, it puts our mind in the right place to focus on metrics that help us think about the future.

DEVELOP KPIS

When choosing a KPI, we need to understand the outcome we are looking for. What am I trying to measure? What am I trying to improve? KPI development has to start with the strategies and objectives you're trying to achieve.

The most common set of KPIs we are all familiar with is the dashboard of our car. You have the speedometer, the gas gauge, the indicator of the temperature of the oil, the check engine lights; some have the direction you are traveling, your RPMs, and probably other things that someone thinks is important. Each item on the dashboard is giving you an indication about some performance aspect of your car. Over the years, car manufacturers determined what to include on the dashboard based on what drivers need to know in order for their car to function properly.

So how do you choose what to use for your microgym? How many KPIs should you follow? Is it a case of the more the better? The beauty of being the owner is that whatever you choose right now can be changed, so please don't feel pressure to get this right the first time. I want you to just get started with something.

If you find that you can't use the KPI to help you make any decisions, you can always stop tracking it. In fact, we strongly encourage you to stop tracking KPIs that aren't helping you make decisions. Hundreds of KPIs have been developed over the years, and many of them aren't going to help you make better business decisions. Let's swear a blood oath to not use any of those.

The sole purpose of tracking a KPI is to give you an indication of how your gym is performing, which, in turn, allows you to filter your time so that you fix the right things. This is why we have to know what questions we want answered before deciding which KPIs to use. Consider how we use our car's dashboard. I tend to pay close attention to the speedometer while I'm actively driving. I often check my gas gauge when I get into the vehicle. KPIs such as the check engine light I only check when it comes on. If I'm trying to maximize gas efficiency, I'm paying attention to my RPMs. If I'm trying to limit how long it takes me to get somewhere, then I'm paying attention to my speedometer. Depending on what I'm trying to do, I'm looking at different metrics on my dashboard.

That's a really important aspect of any KPI you are going to use in your gym. You first have to choose what you are working on. You need to know the destination before you can map the journey. If I'm just starting my microgym, the things I'm working on will be different from a microgym that has been established and is now trying to maximize floor space or is considering the next gym location. That means a startup gym owner is going to be looking at different KPIs then an established gym owner. This isn't to say all their metrics will be completely different. They will probably have a few similarities.

Think about how you teach a gym member the air squat. Because it's a basic movement, we consider it simple. But if you break down each component, we can make it seem over-complicated: plant your feet shoulder-width apart; focus on screwing your feet into the ground, maybe with an emphasis on keeping your pinky toe down; make sure your knees push out as your drop; keep your chest upright; bring your hip crease below your knee; explode up as you engage your quads; flex your butt cheeks at the top; and make sure your hips are fully extended. Each one of those little components could be an indicator you want to look at as you teach your members how to squat. If you ask the member, especially a new one, to focus on every single one of those items, they likely will be overwhelmed and will end up not getting any of them right. So instead, after explaining the movement, you ask them to focus on one or two components, the most important ones for that person. Focusing on fewer KPIs often leads to more efficient improvement. You also know that, based on the member's current skill set or areas of weakness, the few things you ask them to pay attention to will change as they change.

That's exactly how it has to be with your business as well. Don't overwhelm yourself with too many numbers to track. Just pick a few. Usually we recommend no more than seven at a time; many self-proclaimed experts claim three is the best number.

I give you permission to change your KPIs as your gym changes. While there are many KPIs to choose from, below are some we find to be the most relevant to microgyms.

REVENUE AND PROFIT

Two of the basic things that should be tracked are your revenue growth and your net income percentage. These are found on your Profit and Loss Statement (P&L). You want to see revenue grow and you want to compare your net income to the revenue growth. Revenue increases are only good if the net income increases with it. If revenue increases and net income doesn't, you aren't any closer to your noble purpose. In fact, I would say you are farther away because you have a bigger operation, with bigger headaches, and probably more time commitment with nothing really to show for it.

While you should be tracking these KPIs, it's important for you to realize that profit and net income are the consequences of all the other things that are happening inside and outside your gym. Of itself, these are not very valuable metrics. However, combined with the other metrics, you can now better understand why your revenue or net income behaves the way it does.

REVENUE PER SQUARE FOOT

Maximizing how you use your space is important. Revenue Per Square Foot is a good KPI to help you see how you have done so far. To calculate it, take your Total Revenue and divide by the square footage of your space. The higher the number, the more you are maximizing the space.

RENT AS A PERCENTAGE OF REVENUE

Another KPI that looks at how well you are using your space to generate income is your rent expense as a percentage of Revenue. This is calculated by dividing your rent expense by your Total Revenue. According to the *2019 Annual Affiliate Gym Benchmark Report* by Zen Planner, leading gyms spend 15% of Revenue on rent.

LEADS AND CONVERSION

If you are attempting to grow your gym, then knowing where your leads are coming from is important. Are they coming from word of mouth, social media advertising, blog posts, challenges, drive-by traffic? You can even dive deeper into those questions. Is word of mouth coming from stay-at-home moms, veterans, brand new members, gym events? Did a specific communication we sent to our members increase client referrals? Does one ad perform better than another? Does having a guy dancing in a Statue of Liberty outfit bring in more drive-bys? (No. That one definitely won't work).

Next, you want to know how much cash you are spending on each lead source. It's not just about knowing where the leads are coming from, but also how much you are paying for it. "I'm so excited; I got fifty new members this month!" can easily morph into, "Oh, wait, it cost me $50,000 to do that. No wonder I'm going bankrupt."

Tracking where leads come from and how much you spend on each lead source lets you identify which lead sources are the most effective and which ones are the least expensive. Sometimes people refer to this as cost per lead. By knowing that, you should know which lead sources to focus on or improve.

You can't really talk about leads without talking about conversion. It'd be like mentioning peanut butter without chocolate. (No, not jelly, but chocolate.) Once you know where each lead comes from, you also want to know which lead source is easier to convert into a member. Spending $1,000 a month to get forty leads is a complete waste of money if none of those forty leads become members. It makes sense to not only track cost per lead but also cost per conversion, meaning the cost to turn someone who expressed interest into a paying member. You can find a template you can use to track all these at www.ProfitFirstForMicrogyms. com/tools.

These two KPIs, cost per lead and cost per conversion, help you determine your marketing return on investment (ROI). To calculate marketing ROI, you take the income you earn from the member and compare that to either the cost per lead or the cost per conversion. If I make $1,200 from the member and I paid $400 to get that member I would take $1,200 – $400 (which is $800) and divide that by my cost of $400. So two, or 200% ROI. I would then ask myself questions based on that answer. How can I make those ads more compelling? Or how can I pay less per click to get in front of my target audience? Do I need to add something else to improve the conversion rate of that ad? How is my "help first" process? Did I miss a member need which caused me to offer the wrong service? How is my follow-up process with members on their experience?

REFERRALS

Not only should you track all the lead sources, it's important to highlight word of mouth referrals from your members, especially new members. This KPI is simply the number of new member referrals you got in the last week. This is one of the metrics that Lisa Kuecker used with her six locations, and her standard was three referrals per new member. If one of her gyms didn't have at least three in a week then she dug into what might be preventing that.

Referrals from new and current members are the least expensive lead source, and receiving one is a good indication that you are providing a good enough experience to be deserving the coveted honor of having your member tell someone they love your gym. I say, "good enough" and not great because I think we can always do better. We should always strive to improve our members' experience.

PROFIT PER CLASS

Each time you run a class there are costs for running that class, and it's important to know if you are earning enough income on that class to not only cover costs but also have some cash left over (profit). If you aren't covering your costs on a class, then you should cancel the class.

The simple way to think about this KPI is to take the income you earned from the class and subtract the cost of your coach and the other costs associated with keeping the class available. Unfortunately, it isn't that simple. A common way to calculate this is to take Total Revenue and divide that by the number of classes. That gives you an average income per class. Then, take total expenses and divide by the number of the classes which gives you the average expense per class. Next, subtract the average expense per class from the average income per class. You may think you now have profit per class. Sorry. This is like just taking the net income of the gym and dividing that by the number of classes, which is not what we are after with this metric.

Here is the issue: If I have nine members in one class and one member in another class, the previous calculation would say I had five members in each class and probably a small profit. In reality, I had good profit in one class and I lost money in the other. I would be better off cancelling the class with one member and keep my good profit from the higher attended class. I'm not going to know that if I do the previous calculation.

I'm going to explain how one could get the exact Profit Per Class calculation. If you don't really care, feel free to skip the next two paragraphs. The bottom line is that you can get the exact number, but it can be very tedious. How tedious? You first have to figure how much income you make per class, which means you need to know how much income you make per member per class they attend. So if Suzy pays $150 and she attends ten classes that month then the gym's income per class for Suzy is $15. If Kennedy pays $100 and she attends two classes that month, then the gym's income per class for Kennedy is $50. Let's say that in one of the classes during the month, the only two members in that class were Suzy and Kennedy. Then you know you made $65 of income in that class. ($15 plus $50). You need to calculate that income per class per member and then see which members attended which classes to figure out your income for each specific class. Why each specific class? Because the purpose of this KPI is to identify classes that should possibly be cancelled or class times that need a marketing boost.

Figuring out the expenses per class is a little easier. You start with the specific cost of your coach for the specific class, and then add to the coach cost your overhead rate per class, which is simply all your expenses except your coach expense divided by your total number of classes. Now you take the income per class and subtract the expense per the same class. Voila!

This KPI is good in theory but much harder to be super accurate because it has to be calculated on a specific class-by-class basis. That being said, if you have a shred of doubt that specific classes don't have high enough attendance, you will want to run this calculation. Even though I love my three members who always come to my noon class, this KPI will give me a factual number on how much I'm losing by keeping that class slot open.

One good thing is that, if you do this calculation a few times, you should get a feel of a minimum number of members you need in every class instead of having to do the tedious calculation each time.

PROFIT BY SERVICE

This is a KPI that looks at your overall revenue streams, such as group training, bootcamps, personal training, semi-private sessions, nutrition, supplement sales, and apparel. This KPI focuses on how much income each service brings in compared to how much we are spending on that service line.

It's important that we know where our profit is coming from and that we know if we are actually losing money on a service offering. If you discover a revenue stream for which you are losing money, then you should stop doing it or figure out a way to make it profitable.

The ideal scenario here is that your accounting separates these income categories already. For example, you would have a category on your P&L statement that is Group Training Income, and another that is Personal Training Income.

First, you need a separate category for each revenue stream. Then, you need to figure out the expenses that go into that revenue stream. Unlike Profit Per Class, you can't just take a total expense number. Look at the expenses that are directly related to that revenue stream, such as the cost of the team members who are involved in delivering that service. The coaches' cost is an obvious inclusion, but do you have any support staff or outsourced contractors whom you are paying to do something that supports that revenue stream? If you had to buy the item, then you also need to include those expenses (known as cost of goods sold). We have to include any cost you can directly connect to offering that service. Are you doing paid advertising for that revenue stream? That needs to be included in this KPI.

Now you simply subtract these expenses from the income for that service and that gets you the profit by service. You may find that even though you have $1,000 in supplement sales each month, that it cost you $700 just to buy the supplements wholesale, you spent $100 on paid advertising for it, and paid a team member to manage it for another $100. This lowers your profit on supplement sales to only $100.

Another application of Profit by Service is to plan for the future. Maybe you are considering adding a new revenue stream. By estimating the income and direct expenses that would be involved, you can use this KPI to see if you want to invest the time in launching it.

ATTENDANCE

Tracking your members' attendance is important. If you do it the right way, this can be a Key Predictive Indictor of which members are likely to cancel in the future. This isn't just about tracking those who are not attending classes at all, it's also about tracking how frequently the member comes to the gym.

Attendance is a retention tracker. The real secret to growth is not so much getting a ton of leads and adding a bunch of new members, it's keeping the members you already have for a longer stretch. That's where growth comes from. By tracking attendance, you will be able to identify members who are at risk of leaving the gym, because those that use your services are much more likely to value the services you offer. (You know, since they are using them.) A member who doesn't come in very often is likely to think they aren't getting what they are paying for and then cancel their membership. (Of course they aren't getting what they paid for because they aren't coming in.) By identifying that member, you can reach out to them before they reach that conclusion.

So what should you be tracking? Weekly attendance. Do you want to see the entire attendance list for the week? No. The Attendance KPI should report to you members who did not attend at all or only came to one session the last week. Reach out to all of those members.

You may want to track attendance on a monthly basis, and that would be a mistake. A month is too long and would make this KPI a lagging indicator, because by the time you identified which members didn't come at all or came once per week, they probably already cancelled their membership or have made the decision to do that. By seeing these members after just one week, you now have time to figure out what is going on.

NET PROMOTER SCORE

Net Promoter Score measures customer loyalty. You get the data by asking your members two questions:

1. **How likely are you to recommend my gym to a friend/colleague/relative?**

   0 = Not at all likely; 10 = Extremely likely.

   Those who respond 9 or 10 are called promoters. Those who respond 0 to 6 are called detractors. Passive members answer 7 or 8. The Net Promoter score is the percentage of promoters minus the percentage of detractors. So if all your members are promoters, your score would be 100. If all your members are detractors, your score would be –100.

2. **What is the main reason for that response?**
While the net promoter score gives you a number to track
and see if the number gets closer to 100, the answer to this
second question is where the real gold is. Their answer to
why they gave the number will tell you why they are or aren't
referring new members to your gym.

With this information, you can get to work on how to get more of
your members so loyal to your gym that they consider themselves a
promoter of it.

AVERAGE REVENUE PER MEMBER

Average Revenue Per Member (ARM) is an easy calculation. Take
your Total Revenue and divide it by your total member number. If I
did $10,000 last month, and I had 100 members then my ARM is $100
per member.

Our goal isn't to simply take money from our members, it should
be to provide more and more value for them. And the more value
we create for them, the more we should be compensated. Can you
really put a price tag on improving someone's health or increasing
their chance of living longer?

AVERAGE LENGTH OF ENGAGEMENT (LEG)

This is a metric that is a lagging indicator of how well you retain your
members. To calculate it, average the number of days all your current
members have been with you. Breaking that down further, subtract
the current date from the date the client signed up. If you don't track
that information, then you should fix that like yesterday. You have to
track this.

The intention with this metric is to see the LEG always increasing.
While this is a lagging indicator, meaning it does not help you predict
what may happen in the future, it still provides valuable information.
If the number shows that, on average, your members aren't staying

very long with your gym or that the time they stay with you isn't continuing to increase, then you need to focus on retention activities. What are they missing in their experience with your gym that they want? Where can your services be improved? Are your coaches helping or hurting this metric?

LIFETIME VALUE OF A CLIENT

This metric is calculated by multiplying your ARM by your LEG, and it is also a lagging indicator. I know this isn't a popular opinion, but I don't really like the lifetime value metric. I have a few reasons why.

The first reason is that lifetime value is a byproduct, a consequence, of your ARM and LEG KPI. Because of that, lifetime value doesn't really tell me what I should focus on. It could be my prices are too low. It could be we aren't doing a good job sharing how valuable our services are or explaining the options for services. It could also be because our coaches aren't delivering a good service. Or it could be our programming is boring. Or as Jason Brown, owner of Box Programming says, "your members might be leaving because they want to get healthier, not get the crap kicked out of them every day." There are simply too many factors that affect this metric because it is in reality the combination of two metrics. If I improve my ARM, then lifetime value increases. If I improve my LEG, then lifetime value increases. So let's just focus on improving ARM and LEG. Lifetime value will just tag along.

The other reason is that I don't think it is very useful and it can be dangerous to rely on. I'm not a professional researcher. Instead, I go to Google and search terms and related phrases. I read Wikipedia. I wanted to know where this term "lifetime value of a customer" originated because my assumption was that it was created by a marketer. Why is that my assumption? Because the lifetime value of a customer concept benefits a marketer the most.

Lifetime value of a customer is often defined as the monetary value of a customer, based on the present value of the projected future cash flows. (Who even talks that way?) The way I break down that sterile definition is: Guess how long the member will be with your gym; guess the services they, on average, use each year; figure out what they'll pay you for that; and then multiply all those ~~guesses~~ numbers together along with a "present value" calculation. (Let's not waste brain cells even talking about the present value calculation). Seems like a lot of guessing, right?

If you've ever hired a company or person to help with marketing, this is normally one of the first things they ask. They love this number because they like to use the lifetime value number to determine how much you should be willing to spend to get the member. If your lifetime value of a customer is $10,000 based on all that guessing, then the marketing company will tell you that you should be willing to spend up to $9,999 to get a new customer. (If that feels "not right," then you are already seeing some of the problem with this metric.)

The only reference to the origin of "lifetime value of a customer" I could find was on Wikipedia, which some say is not a reliable reference. "One of the first accounts of the term *customer lifetime value* is in the 1988 book *Database Marketing*."[1] Database *marketing*! Guess who's not surprised? This guy! The metric is dangerous because so many marketing consultants put too much weight on it while not asking themselves if there are any flaws in how one determines the lifetime value of their customer. (There are flaws.)

In an article in *Forbes*,[2] a VP of a marketing company demonstrates the danger I'm talking about. He suggested that knowing the lifetime value of your customers lets you know how long those customers stick around and what they buy. He also added that knowing your customers' lifetime value allows you to see whom your loyal base includes. I argue that all the metric indicates is what the business owner is guessing about how long the customer will stick around. It

---

[1] Wikipedia 2019, https://en.wikipedia.org/wiki/Customer_lifetime_value, accessed November 24, 2019

[2] Samuel Thimothy, "Why Lifetime Value Is The Most Important Metric For Measuring Clients," *Forbes*, Dec 5, 2018, https://www.forbes.com/sites/theyec/2018/12/05/why-lifetime-value-is-the-most-important-metric-for-measuring-clients, accessed November 24, 2019

certainly doesn't tell them what they will buy in the future. This is a VP of a marketing company in a credible magazine.

Tracking the lifetime value of a client can be dangerous. There are too many guesses involved. Between now and forever, how long is the member going to use your gym? Having worked with entrepreneurs for more than a decade now, I know that, in general, entrepreneurs are a very optimistic bunch. When we guess, we lean toward optimism. If I've optimistically guessed a member will be with me for five years, when in reality they only stay three years, I probably spent more money than I should have trying to get that member to join.

In my tax firm we use estimated annual revenue (EAR). Please notice the subtle differences between what we call EAR and the lifetime value of a customer. Estimated annual revenue is simply the amount of income we estimate to receive from the client in the next year, and that is solely based on the services they signed up for. We aren't guessing on anything, not on services they may do in other years or for how many years they might be a customer.

It doesn't do you any good to guess how long the customer will remain a member in your gym. What better serves the business is to focus on better serving the member. Lifetime value of a customer doesn't tell you how effectively you're serving the client, or if your messaging is resonating with your audience, or if they like your services. It tells you what you guess they like and how long you guess they will be with the business.

Work toward ensuring your members have an amazing experience with your gym. You control this. There's no guessing needed to know you are going to give your best to your noble purpose. If you can do that, then there is a higher likelihood that the member stays around for a long time.

PROFIT

In the beginning of the chapter, I mentioned it's important to understand the outcome I'm looking for. While I am not a fan of all the guessing that comes with the KPI lifetime value of a customer,

I can appreciate the question they are trying to answer. How much profit can you expect from a member while they are with your gym? As a gym owner, you should know and measure the profit you make on your members. This doesn't mean you don't care about their fitness, or that you can't care about them as people. This doesn't mean you like any one member better than another member; it means you realize that in order to continue to change lives, the business needs profit.

In *Profit First,* Mike wrote, "You can't grow out of your profit problem. You need to fix profit first, then grow. You must figure out the things that make profit and dump the things that don't. When you focus on growth, it is inevitably a scramble to grow at all costs. Yes, at all costs (including the quality of your life). When you focus on profit first, you inevitably figure out how to make a profit consistently."

There are three ways you can make profit on your members. The first is to raise prices on services. Another way is to lower your costs on delivering those services. The third way is to increase the amount of time a member is with you, because that means future income.

Using KPIs effectively is how you figure out the things that make a profit. It's the filter tool that allows you to know when to dump things like classes or services. It's the indicator that tells you what areas need your attention so that you are effectively using your time on the things that will keep moving your gym toward your goals.

The KPIs in this chapter plus the *Profit First for Microgyms* framework will help you focus on profit. Remember, profit is the necessary fuel to a gym's healthy survival.

This is not an exhaustive list of all the KPIs you could have at your disposal. You may find others that work for you. The proper use of KPIs is going to give you a gold mine of actions you can take that will provide positive changes that improve your gyms profitability and your members' experience.

Lisa didn't start off running six locations working only five hours a week. She started with one location and worked ridiculous hours. As she added more locations, and as her hours exceeded what we could even consider "ridiculous," she knew she had to make changes.

It didn't take her very long to start focusing on an infrastructure that would allow her to work fewer hours while still being highly profitable. Every step of the way, she used KPIs to help her assess where she stood compared to her goals and vision.

She had her moments, though. She told me, "My number one financial mistake was not getting right on the financial mindset in the beginning. I ran away from the Profit and Loss statement and the numbers that matter. I just shied away from these numbers in my first couple years, not willing to confront reality. I was fearful because I didn't want proof of what I would see (and taking time to do it was overwhelming.)"

Once she started facing those fears and got her financial mindset correct, she started to excel. She was able to take the profits from the current locations and put them into their next location. By the time she opened her fifth location, she was able to pay cash with minimal debt to get it up and running.

Lisa said, "Processes and systems are absolutely necessary. They were a big part of my success. I learned you have to pay for them one way or another. And still, the role of the KPIs in keeping my hours down and my profits up was everything."

FINANCIAL WORKOUT

Pick three KPIs to start tracking. Your first step is to determine the three most important questions you want to have answered and how frequently you need to see that answer. The questions you come up with should lead you to the KPIs you need to start tracking.

The beauty of KPI reports is that they digest all the financials you may have been avoiding and simplify it into clear numbers that answer the questions you most need answered.

CHAPTER 12

YOUR FIRST YEAR WITH PROFIT FIRST

W HAT ARE THE MOST COMMON REASONS MEMBERS DON'T come to your gym? The unknown and change. What are the most common reason gym owners don't successfully implement Profit First? The unknown and change. No doubt there will be things that come up in your Profit First journey that you didn't plan on. That was certainly the case for me when I became a gym owner, and this is after I successfully ran Profit First in my accounting firm.

When I bought into the gym, rent expense and team member expense represented 114% of income. Let that sink in. What does that mean? They literally couldn't even cover those two main expenses, the two expenses that are most critical to keeping the gym open. Since its opening in 2012, the gym had never had a profitable month. *Ever.* So when I say that I bought a debt, that is exactly what I mean. To keep the doors open each month would require Jason and I putting cash into the business just to pay the two most basic expenses, which is the farthest point from being profitable.

So why take on the debt? I wanted to prove something to myself and to you. I wanted to prove that the systems and advice we had been giving gym owners would work. Full disclosure, I wanted to build credibility for my tax and accounting firm. How many accountants do you know who bought a microgym just to understand their clients better and to confirm the advice they give works? Talk about putting your money where your mouth is. I hear too often people say that you can't make money owning a gym. Ultimately, I wanted to prove that a microgym can make money, and that Profit First works even in a microgym.

I like how Mike explains it. "Profit First works. Period. Whether you use the percentages I provided for you in the [Cash Flow Analysis]… or arrive at your own perfect Target Allocation Percentages, it will work. How can it work with different percentages, you ask? Because your Profit, Owner's Comp, and Tax TAPs are simply targets. You aren't going to start with them, you build toward them. And as you build, you will transform your business into a lean, mean efficiency machine that generates profit on every deposit, no matter how small."

This chapter is all about where the rubber meets the road. I will go over the timing of what to do and when to do it so that your first year of Profit First is as seamless as possible. I can't predict the specific challenges you will face. But I can cover the most common ones so that you will be in the know. Let's eliminate the unknown and the roadblock making changes brings. If you are already doing Profit First, I will also go over how to make the switch to this new refined *Profit First for Microgyms*.

DAY ONE

Mike suggests the first thing you do is to tell your accountant. So, tell your accountant. The last thing you need the accountant you pay who should support you staying in business disagreeing with the magic and beauty of the Profit First system. You want them on the same page with you.

You may need to do some explaining because, unfortunately, the classic stereotype of an accountant exists because most accountants fit the stereotype. Close-minded, uber conservative, stuffy office, mounds of files, smells like cabbage, and abhors change so much that you don't even dare to know how long they've been wearing the same clothes. It's possible they won't open their mind to a better method of cash flow management.

You may luck out with an accountant who gets it from the beginning and will become one of your greatest supporters. However, if your experience is similar to both Mike's and mine, you may be surprised at the negativity coming from your accountant. Do your best to get them on board, and if they can't get there, then find a new accountant. Switching accountants is not difficult at all. Really, you just need your bookkeeping file and a copy of your last filed tax returns. That's usually all that a new accountant needs to start with you. The hurdle is a mental one because change can be hard. If you are looking for a good resource to find a Profit First accountant with experience in the microgym industry, go to www.ProfitFirstForMicrogyms.com/tools.

After you have figured out the accountant situation, you need to set up your bank accounts. In our experience, you already have the OPEX account, because you'll use your existing bank account for this. You will need to set up the INCOME, PROFIT, TAX, TEAM MEMBER, and EQUIPMENT accounts. Then you need to decide if you are going to have a separate OWNER'S PAY account or if you are going to transfer that money directly into your personal account. Once you decide, take the appropriate steps.

The next step is to settle on your current allocation percentages (CAPs). I like to document this by using our Google spreadsheet, a resource that you can use to keep track of your CAPs and that you will also use on your allocation days.

Also, if you aren't sure where to start with your CAPs, check out our free five-day challenge at www.ProfitFirstForMicrogyms.com/5days. It breaks down the process into simple digestible steps and the price of admission is your email address.

DAY TWO

With the bank accounts set up, contact your merchant processing company and switch your deposits so they are hitting the INCOME account going forward. The process usually involves filling out a one-page form that your merchant processor (credit card processing) company will send you.

Next, celebrate! Mike says, "Congrats! I am not saying that lightly. You've just taken a big step. This is likely the first time in your entire business life that you have deliberately accounted for your profit first.

Before anything else, you made sure you addressed your profit, your personal income, and your tax responsibilities. That's a big deal."

WEEK ONE: CUT EXPENSES

Reread Chapter 9 and take action with cutting your expenses. Ask the analyzing questions. (And answer them, of course.) If your business is bleeding money, consider taking a bold stance and applying a band aid or tourniquet by canceling all your credit cards and getting new debit card numbers. I'm not suggesting that you bail on your financial commitments; you simply may not be able to pay them all at once.

TWICE PER MONTH: RHYTHM DAYS

Chapter 7 walks you through what to do on your allocation days. Eating smaller meals more frequently has worked for people to help them avoid feeling too hungry and overeating. The same happens with having two allocation days each month. We reduce the possibility of overspending on unnecessary things. This is also when we pay our bills. Just twice per month. Now we can think about everything else on all the other days of the month.

QUARTER ONE

Regardless of when your day one happens, do these quarterly items on the end of a calendar year quarter. So April 1, July 1, October 1, January 1. The first thing you do is give yourself a profit distribution.

Take 50% of the balance in your **PROFIT** account and move it to your personal account. The remaining 50% will be your safety net in case things go bad, and it really hits the fan. If you have debt, I encourage you to take most of your profit distribution and pay down your debt balances. If you don't have debt, then splurge away! Remember, this is your reward for being the owner, for taking a risk, and for creating value with your gym members and your staff. So friggin' enjoy it!

Another quarterly task is to make a tax payment to the devilish Uncle Sam. I know. It's terrible how poorly our tax dollars are used. Our silver lining is that hopefully you are working with a tax firm that has your tax liability as low as allowable, so you know you aren't overpaying. In the United States, the IRS essentially wants all taxpayers to make payments throughout the year. If you don't, they've given themselves the right to take even more of your money through the form of an "underpayment" penalty. I'm not going to torture you by explaining the rules around that penalty and the exceptions and the exceptions to the exceptions. The simple way to avoid that penalty is to make payments each quarter. Since you are already saving that money in your TAX account, making a quarterly estimated payment won't be a problem for you.

The other thing that you do each quarter is look at your CAPs and see if you can adjust them in your favor closer to your TAPs. Remember the TAPs represent what financially fit microgyms are doing. However, you didn't start your journey with the TAPs. You came up with a starting line for your journey, and now we are another quarter into the race, and each quarter you want to see how much you can move your CAPs.

YEAR ONE

At the year one mark, since you are already doing the quarterly tasks, there isn't really anything else to do. I would, however, suggest you give a little more attention to your TAX allocation percentage. With a year under your belt, you can now more accurately see if you should adjust the TAX allocation percentage up or down.

Also, look at the balance in your EQUIPMENT account. The goal is to get the balance high enough so that if an unexpected equipment need arises, you have the cash available to cover it. Is your balance even higher than that? Now you have some "opportunity" cash. Of course you can keep letting it accumulate for even bigger opportunities. Maybe you are saving for a down payment on a new building. Or maybe there is something out there that is a productive expense worth spending it on. Regardless of what you do or don't do with it, you're in a great position to have the option to choose. Hip, hip, hoorah for Profit First!

IF YOU'RE ALREADY DOING PROFIT FIRST

Early in my experience with microgyms, I assisted 321go Project and Chris Cooper by teaching tax strategies to their clients. During that time I introduced Profit First to them. Many microgym owners saw how Profit First was a solution they could follow. For those of you who helped me pioneer Profit First in the industry, let's go over how to transition to this adjusted version for microgyms.

If you are using Profit First successfully already, whether you follow it exactly or made your own tweaks *and* you are taking your profit first, paying yourself a good wage, basically living the dream, you *do not* need to change anything you are doing.

If, on the other hand, you feel as though what you've been doing is okay and you know it could be better, then let's switch to Profit First for Microgyms.

The three differences are: the additional accounts TEAM MEMBER expense and EQUIPMENT; the target allocation percentages; and what is included in materials and subs no longer includes coaches.

The first step is to add the new accounts on your allocation days.

The second step is to do a Cash Flow Analysis to get your new allocation percentages. When you do this, your OWNER'S PAY and PROFIT TAPs will either be the same or could be less. The reason the percentage could be less is because your Real Revenue is going to be higher since we have removed payments to coaches from materials and subs. So while the percentage may be lower, the actual amount should be the same. Now that you will be allocating a percentage to TEAM MEMBER expense and EQUIPMENT, chances are these percentages are going to be coming from your OPEX allocation percentages, which will be lower because they used to include one of your two largest expenses.

The third step is to continue with your Profit First behavior using the new allocation percentages. As is true with most changes, they seem bigger than they actually are. This is a pretty simple change.

WHERE IS MY MICROGYM NOW?

I am not one of those guys who just shares highlights of my business story with you. Profit First is a great tool and it helps simplify cash flow needs. However, fixing cash flow doesn't automatically change your operations. It doesn't automatically create the processes and procedures. It doesn't tell you how to communicate changes with your members and coaches. We hired TwoBrain Business to mentor us through the process and we hired 321goproject to help us create a clean looking website that has also made building organic search traffic easier. I listened to podcasts such as *The Business of Fitness* with Jason Khalipa, *TwoBrain Radio*, *WTF Gym Talk* with Stu Brauer, Markus Gerzsi's Facebook livestreams, *Seven Figure Box* with Andrew Frezza, and *Ready Aim Empire* with Lisa Kuecker.

My business partner and I experienced our own set of unknowns as we worked on profitability. We didn't know the extent of the cultural problems. It took us more than twelve months to shift the culture to a positive environment and get rid of a few entitled coaches and their crew of members. Paying bad coaches that are just showing up or don't think they should be held accountable to your rules affects your profitability. Bad coaches are also a nonproductive expense because they are not contributing to retaining your members.

From day one we tried to get standard operating procedures (SOPs) in place. In hindsight it makes sense, but we didn't predict the bad coaches didn't want change, so our SOPs couldn't start making a difference until we got rid of them. SOPs improve the consistency of how you deliver services. This improves retention rates which improves profitability. SOPs also improve the efficiency of your team members' efforts. Instead of wasting time reinventing the wheel, they can get straight to using their time productively, which happens to be really good for profitability.

Plugging those two holes took more than a year. I didn't know the previous six years of culture building (or lack of) would take so long to fix. I *did* know it would have been pointless to invest in marketing efforts until these two items were fixed. No SOPs combined with a disjointed coaching staff make any marketing attempt a nonproductive expense.

Using the Profit First system we've analyzed and cut expenses. We're focused on getting to profit because we know we deserve it and our members deserve it. As of writing this chapter, we have only been marketing actively for a few months and have not reached profitability yet. We are finally trending toward it, and the Profit First framework is giving us the opportunity to find it.

Your Profit First journey may take you on a different path. The good news is that all Profit First paths lead to profitability, and, when you find yourself there, I want you to embrace it because you deserve it.

FINANCIAL WORKOUT

Get your accountant on board. If not, go to www.ProfitFirstForMicrogyms.com to find one who specializes in microgyms. You know this system will work and you need your accountant to be supportive of your decision to improve your cash flow system.

Block out the time for your Rhythm Days and treat it like a workout or something else you would never skip. Feel free to earmark this chapter so you can remind yourself what actions you need to take next during your first year.

CHAPTER 13

COMMON PITFALLS

IN THEIR BOOK, *THE 12 WEEK YEAR*, AUTHORS BRIAN P. MORAN and Michael Lennington share how to shorten your execution cycle from one year to twelve weeks. I'd like to highlight their explanation of the five phases of emotional change:

1. Uninformed Optimism
2. Informed Pessimism
3. Valley of Despair
4. Informed Optimism
5. Success and Fulfillment

I can't speak to your experience, but these five phases definitely describe my experience as a microgym owner. When I became a gym owner, I had already worked with hundreds of microgym owners who successfully improved their cash flow with the systems we had taught them. I did not believe I went into this opportunity blindly. I actually believed I understood our gym owner clients. I was optimistic about my ability to turn around CrossFit GSL, and what I learned is that I was uninformed about everything involved. The cliché statement was very true for me, "You don't know what you don't know." It wasn't until six months into the experience, when I came across this chart in *The 12 Week Year*, that I realized I had been in the uninformed stage.

Let me be clear though, the profitable revenue streams I knew CrossFit GSL needed to add was correct. Analyzing the services and determining which, if any, were profitable was spot on. Looking at current expenses to determine which ones were productive and unproductive is a skill in my wheelhouse.

What part was I missing? The whole human behavior and resistance to change part. I was super uninformed about that. I did understand the part about my optimism. I was optimistic that just a few small things could change the gym from barely surviving to absolutely thriving. I was optimistic that the changes I wanted to make would improve the member experience and I was optimistic that coaches would get more enjoyment from helping members. You can imagine it right? Members high fiving each other. A pristine gym that looks as if it belongs in a magazine picture. A gym mascot of a rainbow-farting unicorn. It was a sight to see… in my mind.

I thought I was going to be Marcus Lemonis for CrossFit GSL. If you aren't familiar with Marcus, he has a show on CNBC called *The Profit*. Marcus goes into businesses that need help. Often they either have negative cash flow or their debt burden takes all their profit. He invests his own money and becomes an equity partner. In most episodes, there is a scene where Marcus gathers the employees together to tell them that he made an investment in the business. The employees always seem excited about it. I thought that is how the coaches would react when finding out I was a new owner. Welp. That is not how my story goes.

I was not greeted with excitement, but rather with reluctance and I daresay suspicion. That's when I entered phase 2: Informed Pessimism. I was becoming informed that the changes I wanted to make were going to require the coaches to do new things and provide new services. It would require members accepting that they would need to pay for the classes they were currently getting for free. It would require fighting six years of unconscious bad-culture building. (Your culture is getting created whether you are conscious about it or not.) Do you ever feel as if you are battling with your coaches instead of collaborating? That's how Jason and I felt.

Then came the moment that triggered our Valley of Despair. Over the six months, we identified a coach we wanted to clone. We wanted all of our coaches to be like him. His dedication to the gym was palpable. If something needed to get done, he was there putting in the effort. When a new client signs up, we need to do OnRamp sessions—he took a lot of them. If a coach needed to change the class they signed up to teach at the last minute, he was there. He is also amazing at encouraging members. He can pull the best effort out of them. He is nothing short of amazing. We even offered him the head coaching position, which he never officially accepted.

Well, he sent an email to our general manager and said, "I am going to move on from CrossFit GSL." The email was very professional and polite; it still felt like a swift kick to the teeth. It was heartbreaking for me, and I immediately felt as though I had failed him. I wanted our gym to be a place where an A player like him would enjoy working out.

The despair really sank in because this email came during a week when we opened a suggestion and feedback box for all members to share their thoughts. That feedback was mostly "not positive," and by "not positive," I mean "super devasting to hear." After grinding for half a year trying to improve the member experience and business overall, it was as if all of that time was wasted. Nothing feels more motivating then to hear, "you suck" from your favorite coach and members. Am I right? Yep. Hello, Phase 3, Valley of Despair.

The changes we wanted to make had worked in other gyms, so we had to maintain our optimism that what we were trying to accomplish would work. It wasn't just that idea of working and having a profitable gym that got us through the Valley of Despair. In fact, I would say, that alone would not be enough. It was our vision of having a place that is welcoming to those who need a second chance or a new beginning. A gym where people can count on being encouraged. A place for those who want something more out of life, who know being healthier gets them closer to that "more." We want to give our members the gift of more time so they can spend that time building their own legacies through their own unique genius. That's why we push through, and that's probably why you are pushing through and possibly why you are reading this book.

We stayed the course. We now understood the real challenges ahead and thus became "informed." Because of the strength of our vision, we found our optimism again.

During these five phases of my emotional change, we avoided common pitfalls that happen when attempting to improve profitability. Ron Saharyan, co-founder of Profit First Professionals, often reminds me of the difference between explicit and tacit knowledge. I have no doubt that we avoided these common pitfalls for the same reason the two types of knowledge are different. Explicit knowledge is basically book learning. "I've read about this, so I know what I'm doing." Tacit knowledge is what you gain from practical experience, the things you learn because you put in the time, the nuances that no book could ever properly explain, and the things that make a mentor valuable because they've done this before. How would you feel if, when flying on a plane, the pilot said, "I read a book about how to do this, so you all should be okay"?

What are these common pitfalls? In *Profit First,* Mike lays out the two biggest ones along with eight others to be aware of:

1. **Don't Get Bogged Down in the Details:**
   "First, some entrepreneurs make the mistake of getting trapped in the details, spending hours, days, weeks or longer perfecting their percentages before they do anything. Worse, some entrepreneurs who get stuck in the minutiae never get around to doing anything. It's our old nemesis: analysis paralysis.

   "Perfectionism kills every dream—better to just start." There is a saying: "Nothing changes if nothing changes." If you don't change the way you take your profit, you will never take a profit.

2. **Look Before You Leap:**
   "On the other hand, if you're like me [Mike Michalowicz], you might make the common mistake of taking action too big and too fast. I'm the type who starts before I have all of the information because most of the learning occurs in the doing anyway. But I put success at risk when I go into a situation ill prepared. In those cases, my ego blames the

system when mistakes were simply due to the fact that I didn't put in the necessary preparation.

"The key to successful Profit First implementation lies in stringing together a series of many small steps in a repeating pattern. So take it easy.

"While you slowly start to build up your Profit First muscle, we are also going to get you into a simple, repeating pattern. Entrepreneurs typically manage their money in an erratic, noisy rhythm that causes confusion and panic."

Profit First is designed to take confusion and panic out of managing your cash flow, but it doesn't mean that mistakes aren't made sometimes. Mistakes happen because tacit knowledge is different than explicit knowledge. Someone may be able to read about something in a book, and that will *never* make them an expert (explicit knowledge). Only in the application of their knowledge can one truly learn it (tacit knowledge).

In our tacit knowledge development, we have also seen these eight mistakes that Mike covers in *Profit First*.

1. **Going it alone**:
   Mike says, "Profit First works, and getting an accountability buddy will make sure you let it. Going it alone is the biggest mistake." When I first bought into our microgym, one of the first things we did was repurpose some poorly used space. The gym had a tiny corner that was used as a kid's play pen that would not have been approved by our insurance company. For about $800, we repurposed a spot that wasn't making money into a much better kid area, which would also be approved by our insurance company. This space looks down on the gym floor, is accessed by stairs, and is enclosed by a pony wall. We added a net from the ceiling to the top of the pony wall for added enclosure. That net, that damn net, that friggin' damn net, gave us all sorts of problems. I know zero about construction other than how

to use a screwdriver and how to hammer a nail. During the course of my life I have installed a total of zero nets. I spent hours debating with other people, who had also installed zero nets in their lives, about the best way to secure it for the safety of the kids who would be using the space. The ones that were more confident (not knowledgeable, just more confident) had their ideas tried first.

I went to Home Depot and bought parts, which was like the blind leading the blind. "Is this what they had in mind?" "Sure, that looks about right." "I think." "Based on my zero experience." The first method suggested from a confident, but not knowledgeable, advisor didn't work. Shocker! Then we found someone who had experience installing nets. Their experience was installing nets on bullpens, not from a ceiling to a pony wall. Still, we took the advice because we had no idea what to do and they had some experience. That didn't work either.

After two failed attempts, though, we had a much better idea of what we could do. Finally, we found something that worked. While we eventually got the net up and secure, we wasted a lot of time trying to figure out something I had never done before. It's a given that most people suck at something the first time they try it. How much time could I have saved if I'd found someone with the right expertise? Even if I still wanted to do it myself to save time, getting advice from the right expert would have saved me a lot of time. Who knows, the way they would secure the net might even be better than my end result. An accountability buddy is important; one who has some tacit knowledge is even better.

2. **Too much too soon.**
   Have you ever had new members who beam with so much confidence you know they will likely approach their workouts in a way that exceeds their current capabilities? I was one of those guys. Even though it had been at least five

years since I did any form of physical movement and even though I was 41 percent body fat, I could do walking lunges with ninety-five pounds on my back. "You can scale down, John. Let's not overdo it. In fact, let's try it with no weight, just the walking lunges."

I ignored the suggestion and said, "I got this. This isn't that heavy." I got through the workout. I'm not going to say, "just fine," because my hamstrings were tight and fatigued, but it felt good to work out. And then it didn't feel good, for about two weeks. I walked with the penguin shuffle, and getting up and down from any chair required a lot of effort, and, boy, did sitting on a toilet hurt the ole butt cheeks. I did too much too soon. We see this with Profit First implementation as well. Business owners catch the vision of setting aside profit at the front end and are then overconfident in their ability to use a smaller pool of cash for their operating needs. So they go really big on the PROFIT percentages or OWNER'S PAY percentages, only to find themselves constantly taking from these accounts to use for operations. After so many times doing that, it's easy to think the system doesn't work, so they go back to how they were managing cash before.

The other "too much too soon" situation is not so much making one account too big, but collectively taking all your accounts too big too soon. If your operating expenses need to come down by double digits, then it's important to come up with a game plan on how to roll it out over many months instead of doing it all at once. Profitability is not an event. It's a journey.

3. **Grow first (and profit later).**
"Man, I love this Profit First stuff. This is going to be a game changer for me. As soon as I grow, I'll get started with it." With the Profit First system you can be profitable from the very next deposit. Growth and Profit First are not opposites.

You don't have to choose one over the other. They are, in fact, best buds and want to hang out with each other. Having profit means you aren't using all your cash for your current needs, so you have some left over. You can then put that leftover cash toward growth. If you do not have profit, where are you going to find the resources to grow? Borrow money? You could, but now you just gave yourself a new expense for interest, not to mention a new commitment for your cash needs because you now need to pay back the money you borrowed. Bring on investors? That could work. Wouldn't your gym be more attractive to an investor if you have profit? Yes, it would. The value of your gym is higher if you have profitability. The higher the profitability, the more it is worth. Do both at the same time. Grow and do Profit First.

Before we move to the next pitfall, one more note about debt. Mike explains, "Now, I want to stop right now and make a strong argument for choosing profitability even when you have debt. In fact, when you have debt, you need to be more profitable than ever. Some people say they can't be profitable until they are out of debt, but that's not true. The only way to get out of debt is by being profitable. Debt accumulates because you have more expenses than cash to pay for them, so you borrow." The strong message here is that choosing Profit First will help you with everything else, like paying down debt and growing your gym.

4. **Cutting the wrong costs**.
   Mike continued, "By now you know I'm a frugality junkie. I get a high from saving money, and I get the biggest rush when I find a way to eliminate an expense altogether. Still, not all expenses should be cut. We need to invest in assets, and I define assets as things that bring more efficiency to your business by allowing you to get more results at a lower cost per result. So if an expense makes it easier to get better results, keep it or purchase it. Money is made

by efficiency—invest in it. If a purchase will bring up your bottom line and create significant efficiency, find ways to cut costs elsewhere, and consider different or discounted equipment (or resources, or services) rather than sacrifice efficiency for what you think are savings."

The great news is that if you end up cutting the wrong expense, you can change your mind and add it back. The questions you use to analyze expenses from Chapter 9 will help you avoid cutting the wrong expenses.

5. **"Plowing back" and "reinvesting."**

Here is how Mike explained this one, "We use fancy terms to justify taking money out of our different allocation accounts to cover expenses. Two that are used most often are *plowback* and *reinvest*, which are really just other ways to say borrow. I have done this. I "plowed back" money from my PROFIT account to cover operating expenses, and boy, do I regret it. When you don't have enough money in your OPEX account to cover expenses, it is a big red flag that your expenses are too high, and you need to find a way to fix them fast. Once in a blue moon, it could also mean that you are allocating too much to Owner's Comp or Profit. This only happens when you start with a high Profit or Owner's Comp percentage. And when it happens, it is because you are taking a percentage of profit or pay that you are not yet able to sustain; the efficiencies are not yet in place to support your profitability. But again, this is rarely the reason your OPEX account is in the red. Likewise, some entrepreneurs continue to use their credit cards for daytoday operations and call them lines of credit. This is not accurate. It's money you don't have. Your credit card spending limit is almost never a bridge loan to carry the business for short cash flow gaps (e.g., a big profitable job isn't paying the bill on time as it was committed to). Nope. Credit cards are simply to use to pay expenses, resulting in debt, plain and simple. Using a credit card to cover what you can't afford is also a red flag that your expenses are too high. Stop using the credit card and reserve it for legitimate emergencies or unique circumstances (like for a purchase you must make to yield income). When you find yourself in a situation where you feel the need to "plow back" your profits, *stop* to reassess. There is always a better, more sustainable way to maintain the health of your business. You need to invest thought, not reinvest money."

I also want to emphasize this mistake of "plowing back" or "reinvesting" is not the same thing as using the cash left over after paying expenses for growth. The excuses of plowing back and reinvesting are the buzzwords we use to justify taking money from other accounts to cover operating expenses. When that happens, the gym is screaming at us that we can't afford all the expenses. Rather than take from other accounts, we should focus on cutting the right expenses.

6. **Raiding the tax account**.
   The mistake here comes from the temptation of not having enough cash flow in your operating account to either pay the bills or do whatever activity you want. Because the final tax bill deadline is so far out, it's pretty easy to justify spending money now. After all, we can just save extra later. Right? Are you with me? You picking up what I'm putting down? Exactly. Saving more later never happens. Now we go back to being stressed out wondering if we will be able to cover our tax bill. That is why it is a mistake to raid the tax account.

7. **Adding complexity**.
   The simple way to think about Profit First is that cash is cash. You don't need to worry about how tax depreciation or amortization works inside the Profit First system. You don't need to worry about the miles you claim on your tax return

either. All these items are not cash. Keep it simple. Cash is cash.

8. **Skipping the bank accounts.**
Running Profit First as designed with new bank accounts is very different then running Profit First in a spreadsheet and keeping one bank account. Our natural tendency when managing cash is to look at our bank accounts. That spreadsheet, being stored digitally, is easy to overlook. You aren't used to opening a spreadsheet to manage your cash. You *are* used to checking your bank account balances.

We have gone over the common pitfalls and mistakes of running Profit First. After explaining them, the truth is, there is really only one pitfall. The mother of them all. The one pitfall to rule them all. It's this: Not trying. Just make an effort. Start small and then build on that. The only true mistake you can make is not doing anything.

Chris Plentus, owner of CrossFit Kanna, is a good example of the importance of making an effort and building on that. He started with 1% PROFIT, 1% tax, and paid himself $500 per month when he first opened his gym. Following the process, he continues adjusting and increasing the percentages and he also works on adding full-time coaches and more staff. After about six quarters of a good rollout plan he got up to 5% profit, 15% owner pay, and 7% tax. He started small and was strategic about the way he implemented Profit First.

I could also include stories of microgym owners who made some of these mistakes in the chapter, gave up, and went out of business or stories of microgym owners who overcame these pitfalls and found profitability. I won't, though, because the story I want to include here is yours: How you found Profit First and took these pitfalls to heart and did the only logical thing you could possible do when finding Profit First. You started. You opened the accounts and you started transferring a very small percentage to your PROFIT account. You gained momentum and increased the profit allocation percentage. You're paying yourself a livable wage. You've analyzed and cut your expenses. Your expenses are productive expenses. Your life is better, and you can't help but feel better. That positive feeling seeps into the coaches and the members. Classes are full. Average Revenue Per Member increases, the number of members increases, your profitability increases, and your ability to be around and create a legacy of changing lives increases. And it's all because you avoided the pitfalls, the small ones and the big one. It's just because you simply started, even though you weren't sure how it would work. You just started.

FINANCIAL WORKOUT

Start.

HEALTH IS PROFIT

W HY IS THE TIME THAT PASSES BETWEEN AUGUST 2ND AND August 3rd different from the time that passes between December 31st and January 1st? One is just a "normal" day, while the other involves late night parties, the desire to see the clock actually change from 11:59 pm to midnight, a celebratory kiss, and usually, a resolve to be better.

Does the Earth really know that it just completed another full revolution around the sun? "Hey, I think I'm a year older now! Saturn, let's have a birthday party. Just don't invite Uranus."

Why am I calling our attention to New Year's? Because that is the time of year when most people reflect on what they want in the future. Some even set goals. I give you permission to do that now, no matter what time of year you're reading this. Because you've now been exposed to Profit First, there is no going back. Life will never be the same for you again.

Never before have you had this knowledge about cash flow management. If some areas aren't clear, go back and reread sections. You know that to simplify your cash flow management you are going to add more bank accounts. You are able to determine the health of your gym through a Cash Flow Analysis. You know when to sit down to manage your cash and how much cash to move to your new accounts. To get past cash feeling tight, you also know how to analyze your expenses to identify the nonproductive expenses that should be cut.

Never again are you going to be worried about where the cash will come from to pay your team members. Never again will you wonder how much money you should be making. Never again will you dread the annual tax man. Never again will you worry about your ability to serve your noble purpose.

The best way to make sure you stay motivated is to commit to three key behaviors. That way, if you ever find you aren't motivated to practice Profit First principles, you've already committed to these three behaviors on your schedule, so you have a higher likelihood of finding the motivation again.

The first behavior is sticking with your Rhythm Days when you allocate money from your INCOME account into your other Profit First accounts.

The second behavior is reviewing your CAPs each quarter and adjusting appropriately.

The third behavior is holding yourself accountable.

Mike shared the "secret" of how to get this system to work forever. He wrote, "The premise is simple—we avoid pain and move toward pleasure, putting a significant emphasis on the moment and very little emphasis on the long term. Immediate pain gets the ball rolling, but pleasure keeps it moving. You probably picked up this book because of pain, and you will likely see results quickly because your efforts will reduce the pain. But the only way you will be able to make this work forever is if you get immediate pleasure each time you exercise your new habits. Just as at the gym, the pain of seeing your muffin top in the mirror will only motivate you to work out so much before you decide it isn't worth the effort. The only way to turn it into a sustained habit is to start enjoying your workouts."

Is this what your members want?

What do your members want most? Is it new equipment? Do they want the best coaches? Do they want the best workouts? Are they asking you to provide the best hour of their day? The cleanest bathrooms? Are they looking for the most supportive community from you? What is it they really want?

What they want most is for you to be profitable. In fact, I would go as far to say, they are begging for you to be profitable. Now they aren't saying, "can you overcharge me and jack up prices" or asking, "can you rip me off? Do you just want me to dump money in your wallet?" No. They aren't saying that.

You know as well as I do what they are saying, "I want you to be focused on serving me. I don't want you to be distracted or acting panicked and stressed out because you're strapped for cash." They are saying, "I want to make sure I get your full attention, your full service, your best, because your gym is a place of comfort for me."

The only way you can give your full attention to your members and give them the best service, the best hour of their day, and the best community, is if your microgym is highly profitable.

When your gym is profitable, you can do a million different things for your members—the right things, the best things, the things you know will serve them best. If you aren't profitable, you can only do one thing: Hope to survive.

At the start of this book, we went over common reasons microgym owners give for why their gyms are not profitable:

Myth 1: There's no money in this business anyway.
Myth 2: People don't want to pay that much when they can go somewhere else cheaper.
Myth 3: It's really just a hobby; I don't need to make any money.
Myth 4: I just need ten more members.
Myth 5: I only want to help people, so I don't need to be paid.

These are all limiting beliefs which are kryptonite to a gym owner's noble purpose. And there is one myth that is more damaging than all the others. Profit is a benefit for me, not for my members. Don't buy into that. Profit is most definitely a benefit for you *and* for your members.

You have learned what profit is and how to get it. You learned that to be profitable you have to do more than increase cash; you have to learn how to retain that cash. That is what *Profit First for Microgyms* is all about: holding on to your cash. Not hoarding your cash; holding on to it so that you can use it to serve your own needs and aspirations and serve your members' needs and aspirations. Profit is not about getting rich. It is the necessary fuel for your gym's healthy survival. You can only do what is right for your gym and your members when you don't need to worry about money.

HOW IMPORTANT ARE YOU REALLY?

Let me tell you about Waldo. He was a teacher who ran a moving business during the summer months. That moving business was his gym. He was your average healthy person looking for ways to increase his happiness

Well, Waldo retired from being a teacher and from his moving business. He wanted to increase his happiness and moved his family to Missouri so he could be a retired hobby farmer. This meant he had fewer built-in opportunities for physical activity. So, he essentially retired from his gym as well. And his health started to deteriorate. The effect wasn't immediate, but eventually it took him nearly ten times longer to complete all his farming chores than it should have. Sometimes he would lie down under his tractor, trying to recover from what little physical exertion he'd had that day. In 2002, he needed bypass surgery. It was a routine bypass surgery, and not even on his heart; only on an upper leg. His body didn't recover well. A few days later, Waldo, my dad, died from a pulmonary embolism.

Dad retired from work and exercise thinking it would increase his happiness. When he had his health, he could focus on all the many options to do that. However, once he stopped being active, his health deteriorated and, instead of focusing on any of those happiness options, he could only focus one thing: his health, or lack of it.

While this book is about finding and keeping your profit, it is so much more than that. Your gym is so much more than that. Health is a person's profit. The person who is healthy has a million dreams. The person who doesn't only has one.

We all want a joyous life, an income that supports our definition of success, and a legacy. All of that is rooted in our health. The foundation for humanity is our health. As gym owners, you are the heroes of humanity. I do not say this lightly and I hope you don't take it lightly. You are saving humanity.

Do you know the difference between Waldo and a gym member who attends a gym that isn't profitable? Nothing. There is no difference. They are the same, because a gym that doesn't make a profit will eventually close. You are the heroes of humanity and the only way to use your superpower is to be profitable.

ACKNOWLEDGMENTS

MIKE AND AJ, AJ AND MIKE, I DIDN'T KNOW WHICH OF YOU to put first. I don't want either to feel bad because you were thanked first or second. I love both of you because neither really cares if you get credit or not. So I did what any rational, logical, tax genius, CPA would do and I flipped a coin.

This book would not exist without Mike Michalowicz. Your book *Profit First* has changed my life and obviously was the inspiration for this rendition of your system for microgym owners. I am forever in your debt, friend. And, if I had to guess, I'm probably your best friend.

Anjanette Harper (AJ), you taught me the difference between the "write a book in a weekend" crap and a "top three book" that can change lives. Your guidance has been instrumental in making this book something I'm proud to present to the world of microgym owners.

Many thanks to Amber Vilhauer and her team, who have helped me spread the word so my message can get into as many gym owner's hands as possible. You made the process easy, and I appreciate it. I just had to follow steps. I'd keep going on about many wonderful things about you, but you know how I like to keep things brief.

Ryan "the marketing guy" Vaughn, our beloved Incite Tax booth babe, #winning. Thank you for being a team player and doing whatever needed to be done. I will always cherish our videos we make together.

Writing a book, one that you want to make a difference in the world, is a lot of work. I pulled this off because Heather Harris and the Incite Tax team are amazing at their jobs, which gave me the room to fit in this project.

I'd like to thank HGTV for putting together programming that my wife Cara loves watching. Many a night Cara watched one of her HGTV shows while I worked on this book sitting next to her. Thank you Cara. I will always love you more.

ABOUT THE AUTHOR

John Briggs, CPA, is the founder and CEO of Incite Tax and Accounting, a multi-million dollar tax and accounting firm, which also is the largest firm serving microgym owners in the country. He graduated from Brigham Young University with a Master of Accountancy in Tax. He worked on corporate taxes and trusts in Orange County, CA, with Deloitte & Touche. In addition to earning mastery level as a Profit First Professional, he also has a black belt in Lean Six Sigma. As a well-known CrossFit gym owner, John cares deeply about helping gym owners get paid what they're worth. He lives with his wife Cara and their four children in Provo, Utah. Connect with John at www.incitetax.com.